CAMBRIDGE

T0303165

AMERICAN EMPOWER

WORKBOOK WITH ANSWERS

B1+

INTERMEDIATE

Peter Anderson

CONTENTS

1A WHO LIKES MY POSTS?

1 GRAMMAR
Subject and object questions

a Underline the correct words to complete the questions.

1 Who *did he write* / *wrote* the play *Romeo and Juliet*?
2 Which tooth *does it hurt* / *hurts* when I touch it?
3 What *did it happen* / *happened* after the police arrived?
4 Which basketball game *did they watch* / *watched* on TV last night?
5 Which book *did you talk* / *talked* about in your English class?
6 Who *did he talk* / *talked* to at the party last night?
7 Which student *did she get* / *got* the highest grade on the test?
8 Who *did you vote* / *voted* for in the last election?

b Put the words in the correct order to make questions.

1 you / who / that / gave / book / your birthday / for ?
Who gave you that book for your birthday?
2 parents / to / your / which / did / restaurant / go ?
____
3 Will Smith / of / happens / the end / at / the movie / what / to ?
____
4 did / you and / about / friends / your / talk / what ?
____
5 like / your / first / cell phone / was / what ?
____
6 his / about / was / what / presentation ?
____
7 married / twice / movie / got / year / star / last / which ?
____
8 who / you / to / did / movies / the / with / go ?
____

2 VOCABULARY
Friendship and communication

a Complete the sentences with the words in the box.

out	with	expressing	opinions
into words	~~face-to-face~~	in touch	

1 I prefer having face-to-face meetings with my coworkers, instead of talking to them over email or chat.
2 Marc prefers emailing his coworkers because he can take the time to put his thoughts __________.
3 He got __________ with an old coworker to ask her for some professional advice.
4 Although I left the country 15 years ago, I still reach __________ to old friends if we haven't talked in a while.
5 She works hard and knows how to interact __________ difficult people, so they made her manager of the restaurant.
6 He's not very good at __________ his feelings. He's kind of shy, so I never know if he's happy or not.
7 David's a very direct person. He always gives his __________ about my paintings.

b Underline the correct words to complete the sentences.

1 I *complained* / *argued* / *persuaded* to the server that my food wasn't hot enough.
2 I said I would take a taxi to the airport, but they *complained* / *insisted* / *kept* on driving me.
3 We were *argued* / *encouraged* / *greeted* at the airport by the Minister of Tourism.
4 She *argued* / *expressed* / *refused* to lend him the $300 he needed to buy a new TV.
5 My father *argued* / *encouraged* / *expressed* me to apply for the job, although I had very little experience in that area.
6 My husband and I always *argue* / *complain* / *insist* about where to go on vacation. I prefer the beach, while he prefers the mountains.
7 The babysitter *argued* / *complained* / *persuaded* the children to go to bed at 9 o'clock.
8 The student *admitted* / *encouraged* / *persuaded* to his teacher that he had never tried to read a book in English.

1B I'M USING AN APP FOR LEARNING ENGLISH

1 GRAMMAR

Simple present and present continuous

a Match 1–8 with a–h to make sentences and questions.

1 [g] They play
2 [ ] He's thinking
3 [ ] She's riding
4 [ ] I'm having
5 [ ] He thinks
6 [ ] We ride
7 [ ] I have
8 [ ] They're playing

a a yoga class on Monday evenings.
b our bikes to school on Fridays.
c tennis in the park. Why don't you go and join them?
d about all the things he needs to do before his vacation.
e dinner right now. Can I call you back in ten minutes?
f that his children will live until they are 100 years old.
g chess with their grandpa every Sunday after lunch.
h her bike to work right now because she wants to get fit.

b Complete the conversation with the simple present or present continuous form of the verbs in parentheses. Use contractions where possible.

JUAN 1 Is Emma doing (Emma, do) well at school these days?
PAT Yes, she is.
JUAN 2 ____________ (she, study) languages, like her brother?
PAT Yes, she 3 ____________ (learn) French and Spanish.
JUAN Really? 4 ____________ (she, want) to become an interpreter?
PAT She 5 ____________ (not, know) yet. She 6 ____________ (be) only 14, after all.
JUAN Yes, that's true. And what about sports? 7 ____________ (she, play) a lot of sports at school?
PAT Yes, she 8 ____________ (love) all sports. She 9 ____________ (be) particularly good at basketball. In fact, she 10 ____________ (play) for the school team today.
JUAN Really? Great!
PAT Hold on … my phone 11 ____________ (ring) …
JUAN Who is it?
PAT It's my husband. Sorry, I need to go – he 12 ____________ (wait) for me in the car.
JUAN OK, bye!

2 VOCABULARY

Gradable and extreme adjectives

a Match 1–8 with a–h to make sentences.

1 [f] I hate swimming in that lake because
2 [ ] I thought the book was terrific – probably the best detective story
3 [ ] After we walked 25 kilometers,
4 [ ] They gave him such an enormous portion of spaghetti that
5 [ ] A lot of tourists hadn't picked up their trash, so
6 [ ] I asked her to open the window because
7 [ ] If you're late for his class again,
8 [ ] We all thought the play was awful, so

a I felt absolutely exhausted.
b the beach was absolutely filthy.
c even he couldn't finish it.
d it was boiling in there.
e I've ever read.
f the water's always freezing.
g we left the theater during the intermission.
h he'll be furious!

b Complete the sentences with the words in the box.

tiny impossible ~~fantastic~~ delicious miserable freezing useless filthy

1 We had a fantastic vacation in Bali. The weather was wonderful, the hotel was perfect, and the beaches were beautiful.
2 The weather was ____________ when I was in Winnipeg last week – it was minus 15° during the day!
3 He's renting a ____________ apartment in downtown Paris – it has only one room!
4 The children looked so ____________ when their pet rabbit died.
5 He spoke so quickly, it was ____________ to understand what he was saying.
6 Nobody had cleaned the kitchen for months. It was absolutely ____________.
7 Thanks for a wonderful dinner. The seafood risotto was absolutely ____________. You have to give me the recipe.
8 My umbrella was completely ____________. I was soaked in the rain!

1C EVERYDAY ENGLISH

Well, if you ask me ...

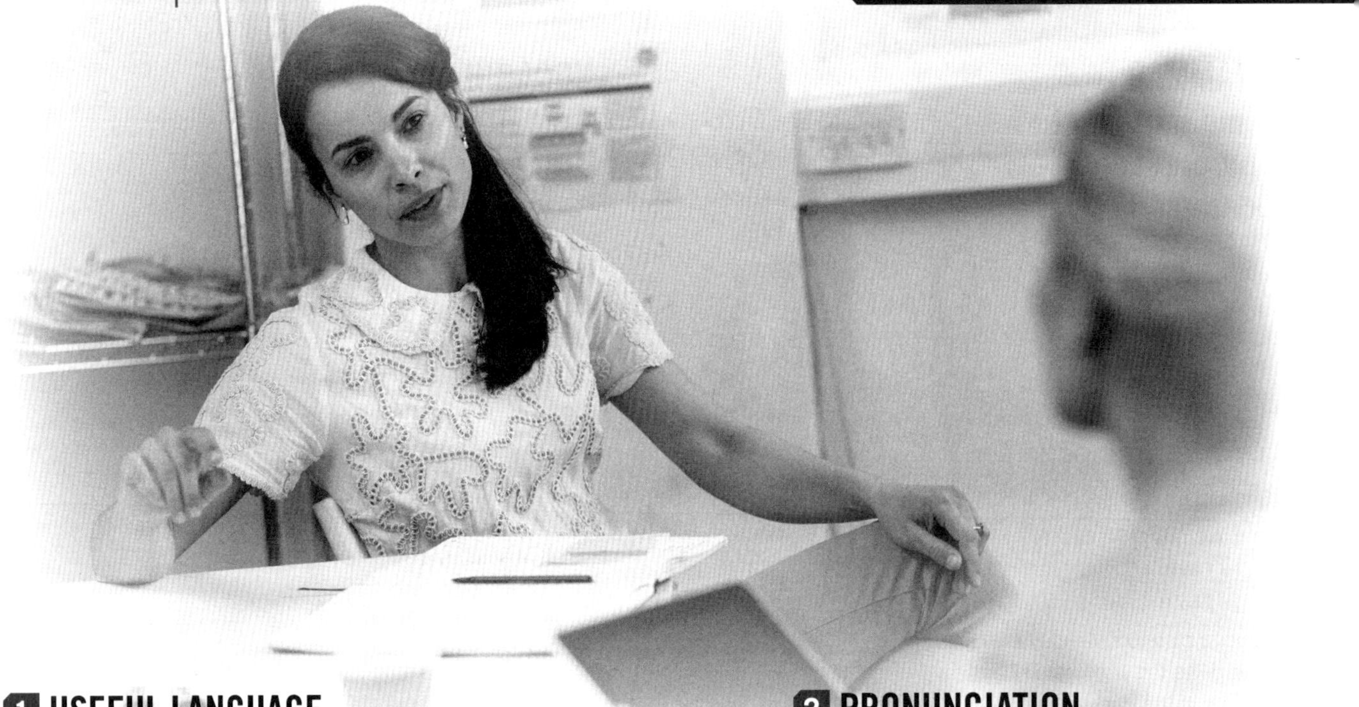

1 USEFUL LANGUAGE
Giving and responding to opinions

a Complete the exchanges with the words in the box.

guess	sure	see	concerned	mean	opinion	~~ask~~	think

1 **A** Well, if you ___ask___ me, Rob Hernandez would be the best person for the job.
B Actually, I don't agree. As far as I'm ___________, Luke Adams would be better.

2 **A** Well, I ___________ you could take the shoes back to the store.
B I'm not so ___________ about that. I've already worn them.

3 **A** I ___________ it's going to be difficult to make enough money to survive.
B Yes, I ___________ where you're coming from. Maybe we should find a cheaper office?

4 **A** Well, in my ___________, Italian is easier than French.
B I know what you ___________. I think it's easier to pronounce.

b 01.01 Listen and check.

c Underline the correct words to complete the sentences.

1 **A** It *comes* / *means* / *seems* to me that their coffee is better than ours.
B Yes, I know exactly what you *mean* / *opinion* / *think*. It's really smooth, isn't it?

2 **A** As far as *I'm concerned* / *I guess* / *my opinion*, I think it makes sense to take the train to Chicago.
B I'm not so *mean* / *right* / *sure* about that. It takes almost three hours.

3 **A** I *mean* / *sure* / *think* France will probably win the World Cup.
B Yes, I think that's *mean* / *right* / *sure*. They have the best team.

4 **A** Well, in my *ask* / *guess* / *opinion*, we need to find another business partner in Latin America.
B Yes, I see *what* / *where* / *why* you're coming from. Maybe a company based in Ecuador this time?

d 01.02 Listen and check.

2 PRONUNCIATION
Word groups

a 01.03 Listen to the exchanges and underline the word you hear before each speaker pauses.

1 **A** Guess what, Toni? I've just read about this girl, and she's only ten, but she's fluent in several different languages.
B That's fantastic. I can only speak one language – English.

2 **A** Hi, Marcela. Are you learning French?
B I'm trying to! But this book's useless! It teaches you how to say "my uncle's black pants," but not how to say "hello"!

1D SKILLS FOR WRITING
Different ways of learning

1 READING

a Read the text and check (✓) the best ending for the sentence.

If you want to be a good photographer, … .

a ☐ you shouldn't take a lot of photos
b ☐ you shouldn't use your smartphone
c ☐ you don't need to study the manual
d ☐ you should always take your camera with you when you go out

b Read the text again. Are the sentences true or false?

1 With a digital camera or smartphone, it is easier to take good photos than it was 20 years ago.
2 You shouldn't use automatic mode when you start using a new camera.
3 It is better not to take many photos when you are learning how to use a camera.
4 Your family and friends will be more relaxed if you take a lot of photos.
5 It is easy to take good photos of people using the flash on your camera.

READ ARTICLE EDIT COMMENT

HOW TO TAKE BETTER PHOTOS

1,843,076 views Edited 5 days ago

These days it is much easier to become a good photographer because of the big improvements in camera technology over the past 20 years. In order to take good photos, you need to have a good digital camera or a smartphone with a good camera.

Make sure you read the manual carefully before you start using your camera. This will help you understand the most important functions, such as how to use the flash and the zoom. Putting the camera in automatic mode is a good way to make sure you don't make too many mistakes while you are still unfamiliar with how your camera works.

It's a good idea to take your smartphone or camera with you everywhere so that you are always ready to take a photo of something interesting. Try to take as many photos as possible. This will help you get better at using your camera and will result in better photos. Remember the saying "Practice makes perfect." The more you practice taking photos, the better you will become.

If you take a lot of photos of your family and friends, in the end, they will forget about the camera and feel more relaxed when you take photos of them. This will help you take photos that look more natural and less posed.

To get the best photos of people, you need to be outdoors, as the light outside is much better. It is extremely difficult to take attractive photos of people indoors using a flash, so it is always better to be outside when you photograph people.

2 WRITING SKILLS Introducing a purpose; Referring pronouns

a Underline the correct words to complete the sentences.

1 *For improving / Improving / To improve* your listening skills, it's a good idea to watch movies in English.
2 You should write a sentence that includes the new word *in order / to / so that* you can remember it more easily.
3 It's better to use a monolingual dictionary. *These / This / Those* will help you to start thinking in English.
4 Some people prefer to write new words on cards with the translation. *That / These / This* technique will help you remember what the word means and how it is spelled.
5 There are a lot of things you can do *in order / so / that* to become a better language learner.
6 Why don't you practice repeating the questions that you hear in the listening sections *so / that / to* you learn the correct intonation?

3 WRITING

a Read the notes. Write a guide on how to be a better cook.

Notes for "How to Improve Your Cooking Skills"

1) Introduction: How to become a good cook
- Try new dishes. Practice.
- Don't repeat same dishes all the time.

2) Learn new dishes
- Buy recipe books.
- Test on family/close friends first. Larger groups later.
- Try new recipes 2–3 times a week.
- Ask family/friends for honest opinions. Make improvements.

3) Watch TV cooking shows.
- Easy way to follow recipe. Watch & copy recipes from website.

4) Share recipes
- Enjoyed a good meal? Ask for recipe. Will discover new dishes & improve.

UNIT 1
Reading and listening extension

1 READING

a Read part of an introduction to a textbook for students. Are the sentences true or false?

The writer of this textbook believes that … .

1 teachers in many countries expect their students to speak perfect English
2 her book is for students who want to improve their English in a short time
3 phrases that seem to be similar can sometimes communicate opposite meanings
4 students may sound rude in English if they do not learn to speak the language perfectly
5 we can understand someone more easily when we think about the culture they come from

b Read the text again. Match the words in **bold** in 1–7 with the things they refer to in a–g.

1 [*e*] By **this**, they mean that …
2 [ ] … **that** might seem strange.
3 [ ] … someone gives **them** a present.
4 [ ] "Why did you get me **this**?"
5 [ ] Why is **this**?
6 [ ] And in fact, **this** phrase (or something like **it**) …
7 [ ] … different cultures say **them** in different ways …

a a birthday present
b ideas that are similar to each other
c people from English-speaking countries
d saying, "Oh, you didn't need to get me anything!"
e speaking English perfectly
f "Why did you get me this?"
g why one phrase is rude but the other one is polite

c Write a short email to the students in your class about learning English. In your email, you should:

- introduce yourself (your name, where you come from)
- explain why you are learning English
- describe where you have learned English in the past
- say what you hope to learn in this course.

Use the phrases below to help you.

Hi! My name's … and I'm from …
I'm learning English because I *want to … / need to … / am going to …*
I have been learning English *for* + [AMOUNT OF TIME] / *since* + [POINT IN TIME]
I started learning English *at school / when I was* + [AGE]
In this course, I really want to improve my …

A BEGINNER'S GUIDE TO
INTERCULTURAL COMMUNICATION

A personal goal for many students is to be able to speak English perfectly. By **this**, they mean that they would like to be able to tell a joke or feel completely confident in a face-to-face conversation with a group of native speakers. Any student can achieve this goal (and many do), but it takes many, many years of study.

If just the thought of all those years of study makes you feel exhausted, then the book you are now holding in your hands may be for you. *A Beginner's Guide to Intercultural Communication* has been written to help students who are learning English answer the question, "What are the best ways to communicate in a foreign language?"

But first of all, let's think about what communication actually means. In our first language, we know that we have to choose our words very carefully. For example, I'm from Australia, so when someone gives me a birthday present, I might say, "Oh, you didn't need to get me anything!"

If you are not a native English speaker, **that** might seem strange. But many English speakers feel it is polite to say this when someone gives **them** a present. However, the same speakers would find it really rude to say, "Why did you get me **this**?"

Why is **this**? After all, the meaning of both phrases is really similar. And in fact, **this** phrase (or something like **it**) is really common in a number of European languages. The answer is simple – whether something seems to be rude or polite depends on culture. To communicate successfully in a foreign language, we need to remember that people are usually trying to say the same things, but we also need to remember that different cultures say **them** in different ways – and that is what intercultural communication is all about.

2 LISTENING

a 01.04 Listen to a conversation between Emily and Noah and check (✓) the correct answers.

1 What is the main topic of their conversation?
- a ☐ the subject Emily studies in college
- b ☐ a vacation that Emily has had
- c ☐ a website that Emily is creating

2 Emily is feeling very tired because she has … .
- a ☐ been writing something in a foreign language
- b ☐ had a lot of essays to write for her classes
- c ☐ just returned from a vacation in Mexico

3 Emily wants Noah to help her to … .
- a ☐ check her grammar and spelling
- b ☐ design a website
- c ☐ improve her Spanish

4 Emily shows Noah a photo of a place in … .
- a ☐ Egypt
- b ☐ Mexico
- c ☐ Singapore

b Listen again. Underline the correct words to complete the sentences.

1 Emily has *just started* / *almost finished* / *stopped working on* her website.
2 At her university, Emily is a student in the *French and Spanish* / *Latin American Studies* / *Culture and Politics* department.
3 Emily's website is for students at her own university and also for students *all around the world* / *in Colombia* / *in Mexico*.
4 *A professor* / *Another student* / *Nobody else* has helped Emily write the information she needs for her website.
5 Chichen Itza is the name of *a building* / *a city* / *a university* they can see in her photo.
6 Noah thinks the photo of Chichen Itza is *absolutely perfect* / *the wrong size* / *too old-fashioned* for Emily's website.

c Write a conversation between two people planning a website for your English class. Think about these questions:

- What information will students need? (e.g., homework, vocabulary)
- How will the information be organized?
- Who will create the website?

Review and extension

1 GRAMMAR

Correct the sentences.

1 What time started the baseball game?
What time did the baseball game start?
2 My brother isn't liking coffee.
3 How was your vacation in Spain like?
4 Look at Tom – he wears his new shoes.
5 Who did take you to the bus station?
6 Can you repeat that? I'm not understanding.

2 VOCABULARY

Correct the sentences.

1 You just walked 20 kilometers – you must be exausted.
You just walked 20 kilometers – you must be exhausted.
2 When we were young, my brother and I used to discuss all the time, but now we've become good friends.
3 It's imposible to sleep because my neighbors are having a party.
4 I haven't rested in touch with any of my old school friends in a while.
5 That cake was delicius, but there was only a tiny piece left!
6 I love that writer. She really knows how to get complicated feelings into words.

3 WORDPOWER *yourself*

Complete the sentences with the verbs in the box.

enjoy help ~~hurt~~ do teach take care of

1 Hello, Grandma. I'm sorry you fell while you were shopping. You're lucky you didn't __hurt__ yourself.
2 ________ yourself to something warm. There's some fresh coffee and tea in the kitchen.
3 Have a great time at the party! ________ yourself.
4 You don't need to go to classes to learn a foreign language. You can ________ yourself using books and the Internet.
5 Make sure you ________ yourself while I'm away. Eat plenty of food and get enough sleep.
6 You don't need to pay someone to paint your bedroom. It's not hard. You can ________ it yourself.

REVIEW YOUR PROGRESS

Look again at Review Your Progress on p. 18 of the Student's Book. How well can you do these things now?
3 = very well 2 = well 1 = not so well

I CAN …	
talk about friendship and communication	☐
describe experiences in the present	☐
give and respond to opinions	☐
write a guide.	☐

2A THEY JUST OFFERED ME THE JOB

1 GRAMMAR Present perfect and simple past

a Underline the correct words to complete the exchanges.

1 **A** How long *were you* / *<u>have you been</u>* at your current company?
B *I worked* / *I've worked* for them since 2017.

2 **A** *Did you ever arrive* / *Have you ever arrived* late for a job interview?
B Yes, last month, because of a delay on the train. *I arrived* / *I've arrived* two hours late!

3 **A** *Did she ever work* / *Has she ever worked* in another country?
B Yes, *she spent* / *she's spent* nine months in our Madrid office in 2008.

4 **A** *Matt applied* / *Matt's applied* for 20 jobs since January.
B Yes, and he *didn't have* / *hasn't had* any interviews yet.

5 **A** *Did you meet* / *Have you met* your new boss yet?
B Yes, *I met* / *I've met* her for the first time yesterday.

b Complete the conversation with the present perfect or simple past form of the verbs in parentheses. Use contractions where possible.

A [1]<u>*Have you worked*</u> (you, work) for a television network before?
B Yes, [2]I ___________ (work) for three different networks since I finished college. Immediately after college, I [3]___________ (get) a job with MTV.
A OK, so can you tell us something about your job at MTV?
B Yes, of course. What would you like to know?
A How long [4]___________ (you, stay) at MTV?
B I [5]___________ (stay) there for five years, from 2013 to 2018.
A Five years? And what [6]___________ (you, like) most about the job?
B I really [7]___________ (enjoy) being in charge of a team. It [8]___________ (give) me some useful experience managing other people.
A And now you're working at Discovery Channel. So how long [9]___________ (you, be) at Discovery Channel?
B I [10]___________ (be) at my current job for two years.
A So how much experience [11]___________ (you, have) in children's TV since you [12]___________ (join) Discovery Channel?
B I [13]___________ (be) a writer for Discovery Family for the last nine months.

2 VOCABULARY Work

a Match 1–8 with a–h to make sentences.

1 [*e*] Steve and Luis both applied for
2 [ ] We've invited four of the candidates for
3 [ ] At conferences, I try to meet a lot of people. It's good to have
4 [ ] She's a manager now, and she's in charge of
5 [ ] Honda is one of the biggest employers in the region, with
6 [ ] He's studying photography in college, and he'd like to have
7 [ ] I've been a teacher for 20 years, so I have a lot of
8 [ ] I have good problem-solving

a a career in television or movies.
b business contacts from other organizations.
c a second interview next Monday and Tuesday.
d experience in education.
e the job, but only Luis was invited for an interview.
f a team of five sales representatives.
g skills, so I can usually find a solution when things go wrong.
h over 2,000 employees in their new car factory.

b Complete the sentences with the words in the box.

grades	apply	charge	experience
~~career~~	team	interview	résumé

1 My uncle had a long <u>*career*</u> in the army.
2 Philip was just promoted. He's now in ___________ of the marketing department at work.
3 I work with a ___________ of five people.
4 They invited me for an ___________ next week.
5 When you write a ___________, it's best to put all the information on a maximum of two pages.
6 I have 15 years of ___________ in hotel management.
7 My brother got excellent ___________ in school.
8 Why don't you ___________ for a job as a journalist?

3 PRONUNCIATION Present perfect and simple past

a 02.01 Listen to the sentences. Which sentence do you hear? Check (✓) the correct box.

1 a [✓] I applied for a lot of jobs.
b [ ] I've applied for a lot of jobs.

2 a [ ] We worked very hard today.
b [ ] We've worked very hard today.

3 a [ ] I learned a lot at this job.
b [ ] I've learned a lot at this job.

4 a [ ] They offered me more money.
b [ ] They've offered me more money.

5 a [ ] You had a fantastic career at CNN.
b [ ] You've had a fantastic career at CNN.

2B I'VE BEEN PLAYING ON MY PHONE ALL MORNING

1 GRAMMAR Present perfect and present perfect continuous

a Complete the sentences with the present perfect continuous form of the verbs in the box. Use contractions where possible.

cry learn go post wait read cook ~~play~~

1 I feel exhausted because I've been playing tennis all afternoon.
2 We ____________ at the train station for half an hour, but my dad's train hasn't arrived yet.
3 She ____________ a lot of messages on Facebook lately.
4 My eyes feel really tired. I ____________ all day.
5 Dad ____________ for hours. He's made an enormous meal.
6 You look really upset. ____________ you ____________?
7 My kids ____________ Spanish for four years, and now they can understand nearly everything.
8 How long ____________ Carson ____________ out with his girlfriend?

b Underline the correct verb forms to complete the sentences and questions.

1 *Dan's been using / Dan's used* his phone a lot recently to take photos of his children.
2 *I've been installing / I've installed* the new program, and it's working perfectly.
3 Have you *been turning off / turned off* your phone? The movie's starting now.
4 My computer *hasn't been working / hasn't worked* right recently. I think something's wrong.
5 *You've been playing / You've played* that video game all afternoon. Can you stop for five minutes, please?
6 How long have you *been waiting / waited* for your phone to install that weather app?
7 *I've been having / I've had* this computer for three years, and it still works perfectly.
8 *We've been trying / We've tried* to call Fiona on her cell phone all day, but she's not answering.

2 VOCABULARY Technology

a Underline the correct words to complete the sentences.

1 You can *download / upload* ebooks onto your tablet and then read them while you're on vacation.
2 Your *password / browser* should be a combination of letters, numbers, and other characters.
3 Please help us save energy by turning *on / off* your computer when you leave the office.
4 I've just found an amazing new *icon / app* that translates pop songs from English to Portuguese.
5 You can *share / delete* your photos with your family and friends on our new photo management website.
6 I think I *pressed / deleted* your email by mistake, so could you send it to me again?
7 If you *click / type* on this button, it opens the program.
8 Why don't you *upload / download* a more recent photo to your profile?
9 You're *clicking / typing* the wrong letters because the CAPS LOCK button is on.
10 When you enter the system, you need to enter your unique *username / icon*, which, in your case, is johnsmith.

b Complete the crossword puzzle.

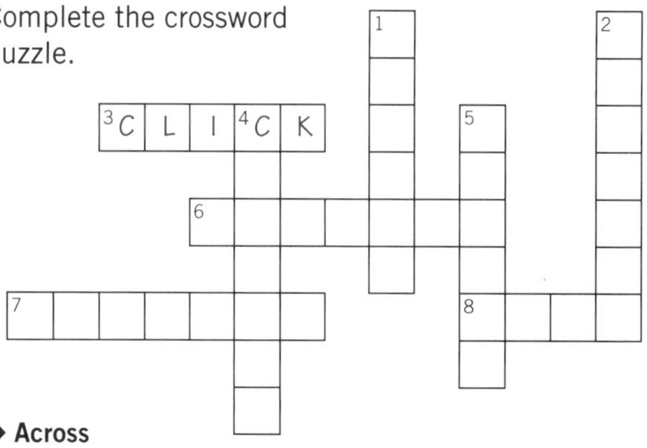

→ Across

3 To visit our website, please ____click____ on this link.
6 If you ____________ this app, we'll be able to use our phones to have video calls.
7 To surf the Internet, you need to have a ____________, such as Internet Explorer or Google Chrome.
8 To log into your account, you have to ____________ your username and password.

↓ Down

1 To use Imagegram, all you need to do is ____________ a photo and select the effect you want.
2 It's quicker to send a text ____________ to your friends than to send them an email.
4 If you are in a café with Wi-Fi, you can ____________ your laptop or tablet to the Internet.
5 If you don't recognize the sender of an email, you should ____________ it, since it might be dangerous.

2C EVERYDAY ENGLISH
Could you take it back to the store?

1 USEFUL LANGUAGE
Making and responding to suggestions

a Underline the correct words to complete the sentences.

1 Could you *ask* / *asking* your brother to help you?
2 Oh, really? That's *terrible* / *annoy*!
3 How about *take* / *taking* it back to the store where you bought it?
4 I'm really *terrific* / *glad* to hear that.
5 Why don't you try *talk* / *talking* to your boss about it?
6 Let's *take* / *taking* it to the garage.
7 Oh, no. How *annoy* / *annoying*!
8 Maybe you could try *ask* / *asking* his girlfriend what kind of music he likes?

b 02.02 Listen and check.

c Complete the words.

DANIEL I'm moving to a new apartment next week, but I don't know how to move all my things. Look at all these boxes!
KATIE How about [1]j<u>ust</u> renting a truck?
DANIEL No, that's too expensive.
KATIE [2]W______ about ordering a taxi?
DANIEL That's [3]w______ a try, but there are a lot of things here. We might need three trips in a taxi. That's not going to be cheap.
KATIE No, it's not. Maybe you could [4]t______ asking a friend to drive you?
DANIEL I'll [5]g______ it a try, but all my friends are students. Nobody has a car.
KATIE Oh, I know! Megan's mom has a flower store, and they have a van. You could put all your things in it, and she could drive you to the new apartment. I [6]c______ ask her to help.
DANIEL That's a great [7]i______!
KATIE Cool! Hey, [8]l______ invite her for dinner tonight, and we can ask her then.
DANIEL Sure. What do we have to [9]l______?
KATIE Great. [10]C______ you go to the supermarket and get some food, and I'll call her now?
DANIEL OK. Thanks, Katie.
KATIE No problem, Daniel. You know what they say. Two heads are better than one!

d Put the conversation in the correct order.

☐ **B** Oh, no. How awful!
☐ **B** Oh, that's great!
☐ **A** OK … No, it's not in there …
☐ **A** Oh, listen – it's ringing! It's behind that cushion on the sofa!
☐ **A** I've been looking for it everywhere. I'm sure I had it when I got home.
☐ **A** That's a great idea. I'll give it a try. Could I borrow your phone for a minute?
☐ **B** OK, so it's not in your bag. Have you tried calling it from another phone?
1 **A** I've lost my phone!
☐ **B** What about checking in your bag?
☐ **B** Yes, sure. Here you go.

e 02.03 Listen and check.

2 PRONUNCIATION Sentence stress

a 02.04 Listen to the sentences and underline the stressed syllables.

1 Ve<u>ro</u>nica just <u>bought</u> a new <u>car</u> and it <u>won't start</u>!
2 My boss has been criticizing my work recently.
3 My neighbors had a party last night, so I didn't sleep very well.
4 My computer's been running very slowly since I installed that new program.

2D SKILLS FOR WRITING
I'm going to look for a new job

1 READING

a Read the email and check (✓) the correct answer.

a ☐ Francesca has found a job with an advertising agency in Los Angeles.
b ☐ Francesca is going to join a rock band in Los Angeles.
c ☐ Francesca is going to begin her new job in Los Angeles in April.
d ☐ Francesca is going to work in a hotel in Hollywood.

Hi Anna,

I'm sorry I didn't reply to your last email right away, but I've been very busy for the last two weeks.

I've been traveling from Orange County to Los Angeles most days for job interviews. I've had interviews with some major advertising agencies and marketing companies, and it's been great to make so many business contacts in Los Angeles.

You'll never believe this, but Outreach Marketing just emailed me to offer me a job at their offices in Hollywood. The job sounds amazing! They want me to be in charge of a team that helps promote some well-known pop stars and rock bands. And what's really amazing is that they also want me to find new singers and bands that we could promote in the future.

They've made me a fantastic job offer. Apart from giving me a really good salary, they're also going to give me a company car. But the best thing is that they've agreed to pay for me to stay in a hotel in Hollywood for a month while I look for an apartment to rent. Besides going to a lot of concerts, I'll also be able to visit all the museums and art galleries I've read about. I've accepted the offer and am going to start my new job at the beginning of April. I can't wait!

Everyone says that Los Angeles is a fantastic city, so I'm really looking forward to living there. We have to get together before I leave, so why don't we meet up for coffee in the next two or three weeks? Let me know a day that works for you.

See you soon,

Francesca

b Read the email again. Are the sentences true or false?

1 Francesca has been to Los Angeles several times in the last two weeks.
2 Francesca didn't meet any important people in Los Angeles.
3 Francesca is going to be a manager at a marketing company.
4 Outreach Marketing isn't interested in promoting new singers or bands.
5 Francesca has already found an apartment to rent in Los Angeles.
6 Francesca thinks that it will be nice to live in Los Angeles.

2 WRITING SKILLS
Adding new information

a Match 1–6 with a–f to make sentences.

1 [f] Besides its wonderful beaches,
2 ☐ In addition to my teaching experience in Canada,
3 ☐ Apart from Flexi Airlines,
4 ☐ Besides agreeing to pay for four flights back to the U.K. each year,
5 ☐ I have excellent technical qualifications.
6 ☐ Apart from paying me a higher salary, they're

a I've worked as a pilot for an American airline.
b In addition, I speak three languages fluently.
c they've also agreed to pay for my family to fly to Dubai once a year.
d also going to give me a company car.
e I've also worked at an elementary school in South Africa for two years.
f Sicily also has a lot of interesting historical sites.

3 WRITING

a Read the notes. Write an email to Martina, a friend you haven't talked to recently.

Notes for email to Martina

1) Apology for not replying sooner.
2) Wrote new book. Sent to New York publishing companies. Been offered contract.
3) Asked to make changes. More interesting for young people. Will work with editor.
4) Will pay me a lot of money. Can stop teaching & spend all my time writing.
5) Best part – going to California. First trip to the West Coast. Meeting editors & Hollywood movie producers. Might make it into a movie.
6) Dinner together next week? New Italian restaurant downtown. Want to try?

UNIT 2
Reading and listening extension

1 READING

a Read the website and check (✓) the correct answers.

1 Where might you see a text like this?
 a ☐ in a book of short stories
 b ☐ in a college textbook
 c ☐ on a college website

2 What is the main purpose of this text?
 a ☐ to explain how to control lights in a building
 b ☐ to give people facts about the camp
 c ☐ to persuade students to come to the camp

3 What is the main purpose of the student stories?
 a ☐ to show that students can have fun while they learn
 b ☐ to show that the camp can help your future career
 c ☐ to show that the camp leaders are helpful

4 When did Dan and Kristen write their student stories?
 a ☐ before the camp
 b ☐ during the camp
 c ☐ after the camp

b Read the website again and check (✓) the correct answers.

Who … ?	Dan	Kristen	Neither Dan nor Kristen
1 has been to the camp before		✓	
2 says the camp is not the same as their normal education			
3 felt unhappy at the beginning of the camp			
4 is going to college soon			
5 says they have improved their problem-solving skills			
6 surprises people in their hometown with their knowledge of computers			
7 was told about the camp at their school			
8 prefers camp because they do not enjoy their normal school			
9 has a busy social life in their hometown			
10 mentions something they have been making at the camp			

c Write a "student story" for a course you are taking. Include the following:

- how you felt about the course before you began
- how you feel about the course now
- what kind of things you have been doing (or did) in the course
- why you think other people might enjoy the course.

CODING CAMP

ABOUT

Since 1978, Upper Canada College (UCC) has been providing educational and fun summer camps to kids. We are proud to bring back our coding camp for its fourth year! It's for students ages 12 to 17 who want to learn and have a lot of fun at the same time.

STUDENT STORIES

Dan Austin from Toronto, 15

This is my first time, so I didn't know what to expect. I've been having a really amazing time though, and I really want to come back again. It's completely different from school, and that's something I really like about the camp.

I've always gotten the highest grades in everything at my high school, especially in math. It was my math teacher who told me about the camp. She persuaded my dad that it could help me get a career in IT. I guess that must be true, and I'm pretty sure that's why my dad let me come here, but I'm just having fun!

This week, I've been working on a program that can control the lights in a building. It's been really cool, and I love working with kids who are just like me.

Kristen Berg from Brampton, 17

I've been coming to the UCC Computer Camp since I was 14, so this is my third time here. There's no doubt about it – this is one of the coolest things you can do during summer vacation.

Some people back in Brampton are really surprised that I know so much about computers. They don't expect me to know anything about them because I'm a girl with long blond hair and I love music, dancing, and going out with friends. But, of course, they're wrong! Every camp has been great, and I've learned so much here. In fact, I want to study computer science in college next year and then work in robotics after I graduate.

2 LISTENING

a 02.05 Listen to part of a job interview. Put the topics from the interview in the order that you hear them.

- ☐ a practical skill someone has learned at work
- ☐ high school education
- ☐ an ability the employers think is useful
- ☐ work experience
- ☐ a qualification from college
- ☐ the place where one speaker was born
- [1] how the interview will be organized

b Listen to the interview again and check (✓) the correct answers.

1 Carlos came to the interview … .
a ☐ by car b ☐ by plane c ☑ by train

2 How old is Carlos?
a ☐ 23 b ☐ 24 c ☐ 25

3 Where did Carlos study computer science?
a ☐ in Spain b ☐ in San Francisco
c ☐ in Philadelphia

4 How many languages does Carlos speak?
a ☐ 2 b ☐ 3 c ☐ 4

5 When Carlos says he is "a people person," he means that … .
a ☐ he can work with other people easily
b ☐ he has a specialist knowledge of people
c ☐ his family comes from different countries

6 What does Carlos do at his current job?
a ☐ He creates apps for cell phones.
b ☐ He sells cell phones.
c ☐ He teaches computer languages.

c Look at the job ad below. Write a conversation between two people. Person A is interviewing Person B for the job of team leader. Use these questions to help you:

- Can you tell us about yourself? (name, age, work/study)
- What experience do you have that would be helpful for this job?
- Why do you think you would be a good team leader? (Person B gives reasons)

TEAM LEADER FOR INTERNATIONAL YOUTH SUMMER CAMP

Every year, Upper Canada College (UCC) provides an International Youth Summer Camp for 600 children ages 12 to 17 from countries all around the world. The purpose of the camp is to:
- develop self-confidence and creative thinking
- teach problem-solving skills
- give opportunities to practice practical skills with technology
- let them have fun!

We are looking for people to be team leaders. Team leaders must:
- speak English and at least one other language
- have a positive attitude
- have knowledge about a sport, skill, or hobby that will help students learn self-confidence, creative thinking, and problem-solving or practical skills.

Review and extension

1 GRAMMAR

Correct the sentences. Use contractions where possible.

1 Did you ever gone to Australia?
Have you ever gone to Australia?
2 I can't talk to Julia because she's talked on the phone all day.
3 I've been to Portugal on vacation three years ago.
4 I've been knowing Jack for about five years.
5 His train has been late this morning, so he just arrived.
6 Last night she has gone to the party with her sister.
7 He works as a taxi driver since 2008.
8 She has red eyes because she's cried.

2 VOCABULARY

Correct the sentences.

1 She's the manager of a game of five sales representatives.
She's the manager of a team of five sales representatives.
2 Please turn out your phones because the movie is about to start.
3 Can you give me your password so I can connect to Internet?
4 I have a lot of experiences managing people.
5 My brother just sent me a text massage to say he'll be late.
6 Sarah applied the job at the hospital, but she didn't get it.
7 The English keyboard is different from the one in my language, so I keep making mistakes when I press.
8 My brother just got a new work with a large bank in London.

3 WORDPOWER *look*

<u>Underline</u> the correct words to complete the sentences.

1 I think we're lost. Let's look *after* / <u>*at*</u> / *out* the map so we can see where we are.
2 Can I help you? Yes, we're looking *after* / *for* / *out* a hotel.
3 Why don't you look *at* / *out* / *up* the phone number of the restaurant online?
4 I'm really looking *after* / *for* / *forward* to meeting you.
5 Shall we look *after* / *around* / *out* the old town to see if there are any nice places to eat?
6 Look *at* / *for* / *out*! There's an old lady crossing the road!

REVIEW YOUR PROGRESS

Look again at Review Your Progress on p. 30 of the Student's Book. How well can you do these things now?
3 = very well 2 = well 1 = not so well

I CAN …	
talk about experiences of work and training	☐
talk about technology	☐
make and respond to suggestions	☐
write an email giving news.	☐

3A SHE HAD MOVED THERE 20 YEARS EARLIER

1 GRAMMAR Narrative tenses

a Underline the correct words to complete the sentences.

1 By the time we *were getting* / *had gotten* / *got* to the park, it *had started* / *started* / *was starting* snowing heavily, so we *were making* / *made* / *had made* a snowman.
2 While he *cleaned* / *had cleaned* / *was cleaning* the window above the door, he *had fallen* / *fell* / *was falling* off the chair and *broke* / *was breaking* / *had broken* his leg.
3 By the time it *stopped* / *had stopped* / *was stopping* raining, it *was* / *was being* / *had been* too late to go to the beach.
4 When the two police officers *were ringing* / *rang* / *had rung* my doorbell, I *was having* / *had* / *had had* dinner.
5 Michelle *was meeting* / *met* / *had met* him in 2017 while she *was working* / *worked* / *had worked* in Quito.
6 When I *was seeing* / *had seen* / *saw* Mario yesterday, he *looked* / *was looking* / *had looked* sad because his pet rabbit *escaped* / *had escaped* / *was escaping* the day before.
7 They *talked* / *were talking* / *had talked* about the accident when the ambulance *had arrived* / *was arriving* / *arrived*.

b Complete the sentences with the simple past, the past continuous, or the past perfect forms of the verbs in parentheses.

1 He ___met___ (meet) his girlfriend while they __________ (study) together at Brown University.
2 We __________ (leave) Barcelona on Monday morning, and by Wednesday evening, we __________ (cycle) 275 kilometers.
3 By the time the police __________ (arrive), the bank robbers __________ (escape) in their car.
4 This morning, she __________ (ride) her bike around the lake and __________ (take) photos of the birds.
5 She __________ (hear) the fireworks while she __________ (watch) TV.
6 The car __________ (crash) into the tree while they __________ (cross) the road.
7 The restaurant __________ (close) by the time we __________ (get) there.
8 Ibrahim __________ (call) me while he __________ (wait) for his flight.

2 VOCABULARY Relationships

a Match 1–5 with a–e to make sentences and questions.

1 [d] I've always had a good
2 [ ] They come from the same
3 [ ] I know he's shy at first, but once you get to
4 [ ] Who do you get
5 [ ] I have quite a few things

a along with best – your brother or your sister?
b in common with Jack. For example, we both like rap music.
c background. Both of their families were farmers in Ohio.
d relationship with both of my parents.
e know him, he can be very sociable and funny.

b Complete the sentences with the words in the box.

calm ~~touch~~ friendship open-minded old-fashioned prejudiced

1 It's easy to keep in ___touch___ with your family when you go on a business trip – you can send emails and texts and even have video chats.
2 Our __________ is really important to us. We've known each other since we were five years old.
3 Eva and Andrés have very different styles. Andrés is modern, while Eva is a little __________.
4 Although Ben's grandma used to be very conservative, recently she's become more __________. She asks a lot of questions and listens to Ben's opinions.
5 Whenever I'm feeling worried, I talk to my mom. She's so __________ and easygoing – she always makes me feel better!
6 James can be really __________ sometimes. He said he didn't like Mike before he even got to know him.

3 PRONUNCIATION Linking sounds

a 03.01 Listen to the sentences. Underline the linked words where one word ends in a consonant sound and the next word starts with a vowel sound.

1 Mark and Ali got to know each other when they worked in Ecuador.
2 They have a lot in common.
3 He gets along really well with his aunt.
4 I'm not very good at keeping in touch with old friends.
5 Most of my friends come from the same background.

3B PEOPLE USED TO MIX US UP ALL THE TIME

1 GRAMMAR *used to, usually*

a Underline the correct words to complete the sentences.

1. Our family *usually gets together* / *used to get together* on Sundays. It's nice to keep in touch with everyone.
2. These days, I *usually walk* / *used to walk* to work – it's much healthier.
3. When I was seven, my parents *usually send* / *used to send* me to stay with my grandparents in Scotland for six weeks.
4. *Do you usually get* / *Did you used to get* along well with your teachers when you were in high school?
5. She *doesn't usually like* / *didn't use to like* tea or coffee when she was little.
6. When I was a little girl, I *usually hang out* / *used to hang out* with my cousin and her friends a lot.
7. Since I was an only child, I *didn't use to have* / *don't usually have* anyone to play with on vacation.
8. *Did you used to take* / *Do you usually take* the bus to work when it rains?

b Complete the article with the verbs in the box and the correct form of *used to* or the simple present.

drive	live	go	sit	eat

Before Jason won the lottery two years ago, he 1 used to live in a small apartment next to the bus station. Now he 2__________ in an enormous house with a swimming pool and a tennis court. Jason 3__________ a 15-year-old car, but these days, he 4__________ a brand new Ferrari. Before winning the lottery, he hardly ever 5__________ on vacation, but nowadays, he usually 6__________ on vacation to places like Bali and the Caribbean. On hot summer days, Jason 7__________ in the park, but these days, he usually 8__________ by the swimming pool in his huge backyard. When Jason didn't have a lot of money, he 9__________ in restaurants very often, but now he usually 10__________ in expensive restaurants three or four times a week.

2 VOCABULARY Multi-word verbs

a Match 1–8 with a–h to make sentences.

1 [f] When I was a teenager, I used to hang
2 [ ] John's got a great sense of humor. I think he takes
3 [ ] After I left home, my parents started to grow
4 [ ] In *The Jungle Book*, Mowgli was brought
5 [ ] Megan wanted a change for the summer, so she cut
6 [ ] Although José and I come from very different backgrounds, I get
7 [ ] All the students from my old class get
8 [ ] Most people think that I'm English, but I actually grew

a off her long blond hair!
b up by a family of wolves. It's an incredible story.
c up in Ireland and then came to live in London after graduating.
d together every two or three years for a reunion party.
e after his grandpa, who was always telling jokes.
f out with my older brother and his friends.
g apart, and two years later, they got divorced.
h along with him really well, and we have great conversations.

3C EVERYDAY ENGLISH

You won't believe what I did!

1 USEFUL LANGUAGE

Telling a story

a Complete the sentences with the words in the box.

matters turned anyway end
won't guess ~~thing~~ funny

1 The best *thing* is that my new apartment is air conditioned.
2 ________, we still hadn't found a hotel for my grandparents.
3 In the ________, we bought him a video game.
4 It ________ out that he had never played golf in his life.
5 You'll never ________ what Sophia said to David.
6 The ________ thing was that he didn't know she was joking.
7 You ________ believe what he bought her for her birthday. A snake!
8 To make ________ worse, the water was too cold to take a shower.

b 03.02 Listen and check.

c Put the words in the correct order to make sentences.

1 guess / you'll / happened / the / what / party / never / at .
You'll never guess what happened at the party.
2 best / has / pool / thing / that / the / it / swimming / a / is .
____
3 Maria / we still / find / had / to / a / anyway, / for / present .
____
4 heavily / worse, / make / raining / to / it / matters / started .
____
5 did / you / believe / Saturday / I / on / what / won't .
____
6 funny / the / what / realize / thing / was / she / that / didn't / happened / had .
____
7 in / us / end, / the / he / to drive / home / agreed .
____
8 ticket / it / out / had / that / turned / train / she / her / lost .
____

d 03.03 Listen and check.

2 PRONUNCIATION

Stress in word groups

a 03.04 Listen to the sentences and underline the words before the speakers pause.

1 But anyway, the train was still at the station, and we got on just as the doors were closing.
2 In the end, we went to a little restaurant near the station, where we had a wonderful dinner.
3 To make matters worse, the server dropped the tray of food, and it ruined my new white dress.
4 On top of that, when she eventually got to the airport, they told her that her flight was almost two hours late.
5 Anyway, in the end, I found a beautiful apartment downtown, and the best thing is that it's only a thousand dollars a month!

b Listen to the sentences again and underline the stressed syllables.

1 But anyway, the train was still at the station, and we got on just as the doors were closing.
2 In the end, we went to a little restaurant near the station, where we had a wonderful dinner.
3 To make matters worse, the server dropped the tray of food, and it ruined my new white dress.
4 On top of that, when she eventually got to the airport, they told her that her flight was almost two hours late.
5 Anyway, in the end, I found a beautiful apartment downtown, and the best thing is that it's only a thousand dollars a month!

3D SKILLS FOR WRITING
He wanted to see the world

1 READING

a Read the email and check (✓) the correct answer.

a ☐ Jack played professional soccer in the 1980s.
b ☐ Jack played for Newcastle United for five years.
c ☐ Jack joined Newcastle United in 1973.
d ☐ Jack scored 100 goals for the factory team.

b Read the email again. Are the sentences true or false?

1 Paolo's and Carla's uncle used to be a professional soccer player.
2 When Jack was 16, he played for Newcastle United.
3 Jack was still playing professional soccer in the 1980s.
4 Jack and Giulia got married two years after they met.
5 Jack and Giulia died in 2012.

Hi Carla,

I've been talking to Dad about our family history, and I've found out some interesting things about his brother Giacomo, our Uncle Jack. Well, apparently, he was a professional soccer player for a few years in the 1970s!

Jack left school at 16 in 1968 and worked at a car factory in Newcastle for five years. While he was working there, he used to play soccer every Saturday for the factory team. One day, some men from Newcastle United came to watch him. They offered him a contract, so in 1973, Jack left the car factory and became a professional soccer player. Apparently, he played for Newcastle United from 1973 until 1979 and scored over 100 goals for them. However, he broke his leg badly in 1979 and had to give up playing professional soccer.

After that, he got a job as a soccer coach at a local high school, and that's where he met his wife, Auntie Giulia. She was an art teacher. They fell in love and got married two years later, in 1981. Our cousins Luigi and Anna were born in 1982 and 1984. As you know, we left Great Britain and came to live here in New Jersey in 1985, so it was hard for Dad and Uncle Jack to keep in touch after that.

Meanwhile, in 1989, Uncle Jack and Auntie Giulia opened an Italian restaurant called *La Forchetta* in downtown Newcastle. For the next 20 years, this was the most popular Italian restaurant in Newcastle. Sadly, in 2012, Uncle Jack was killed in a car accident, and Auntie Giulia decided to sell the restaurant.

When I travel to the U.K. on business later this year, I'm planning to meet our cousins, Luigi and Anna.

Hope to see you soon,

Paolo

2 WRITING SKILLS Describing time

a Match 1–6 with a–f to make sentences.

1 [f] She lived in Buenos Aires for
2 ☐ He continued studying until he was 22. Meanwhile,
3 ☐ He visited the Grand Canyon during
4 ☐ Uncle Julian was a major in the army from 1995
5 ☐ She worked as a receptionist over
6 ☐ My parents met a long time ago while

a his first business trip to the U.S.
b his twin brother was working at the family's shoe factory.
c they were both teaching English in Indonesia.
d the summer, when it was particularly busy.
e until his retirement a few years ago.
f seven years before moving to Texas.

3 WRITING

a Read the notes. Imagine your grandfather was James Cooper. Write his biography.

Notes for biography of James Cooper (Grandpa)

Introduction: James Cooper (Grandpa). My sister and I really close to him. Remember lunch with grandparents every Sunday when young. Always made us laugh – a lot of jokes and funny stories.

Life story:
1938 Born Burlington, Vermont. Very happy childhood. 1 brother & 2 sisters.
1946 Family moved to Montreal. Stayed there 10 years. Spoke English and French.
1956–1962 Studied medicine at Johns Hopkins University.
1962 Graduated from Johns Hopkins.
1963–1972 Worked in different hospitals in Maryland.
1972–1985 Job in hospital in San Francisco. Met Elspeth Clark (Grandma).
1974 Married Elspeth.
1975 My mother born. No other children.
1985–1990 Job in Johannesburg, South Africa. Friendship with famous heart surgeon Christiaan Barnard.
1998 Retired aged 60.
2010 Died aged 72. Miss him very much.

UNIT 3
Reading and listening extension

1 READING

a Read the text and check (✓) the correct answers.

1 This text comes from … .
   a ☐ a newspaper article
   b ☐ a novel
   c ☐ an essay

2 Which of these adjectives best describes the text?
   a ☐ amusing   b ☐ romantic   c ☐ strange

3 What is the best way to describe what happens in this text?
   a ☐ A student cannot complete an essay because of a noise outside her room.
   b ☐ A student is trying to complete an essay when something unusual happens.
   c ☐ A student is waiting for her friends to call her, but they come to her house instead.

4 In the text, what is compared to "a busy teacher"?
   a ☐ a clock   b ☐ a computer   c ☐ a drawer

5 In the text, what is compared to "a dog's nose"?
   a ☐ the curtains   b ☐ the rain   c ☐ the streets

b The order of the events in the story is different from the order that the events happened. Read the text again and put the events in the order they happened.

☐ Jen started writing her essay.
☐ It stopped raining.
☐ Jen had a big shock.
☐ A voice called Jen's name.
1 It started raining.
☐ Jen heard a noise outside.
☐ The group hid from Jen.
☐ Jen turned her computer on.

c Write a short story that begins with this sentence: *I had just arrived at the movie theater when Andrea called.*

Jen sighed heavily. She hadn't done anything for at least ten minutes. She looked at the clock, and the clock looked back at her. It was like a busy teacher: "tick, tick, tick ..." It ticked every second, and the seconds became minutes. Jen sighed again, even more heavily this time.

"You're no friend of mine," she said, picking up the noisy clock. She walked to the other side of her bedroom, opened a drawer, threw the clock in, and closed the drawer again. Jen went back to her computer to do some more sighing. None of her friends were online, and she had at least another 500 words to write.

Suddenly, there was a noise from outside. Jen went over to the window, opened the curtains just a little bit, and put one eye very carefully against the window. It had been raining that day, and the streets were as cold, black, and wet as a dog's nose. She couldn't see very clearly, but she could hear them.

There was a group of maybe seven or eight figures all hanging out together. She checked her phone – no one had sent her a text in the last five minutes. She looked at the computer – everyone she knew was still offline. So who were they?

The laughing and shouting from outside had become much louder, so Jen went to the curtains for another look. As soon as she opened the curtains, everything went quiet.

"That's strange," she thought. The whole group had disappeared. She listened more carefully, but there was only silence.

"JEN! JEN!! WE CAN *SEE* YOU, JEN!!!" eight voices shouted at once.

There was a feeling like someone had poured a glass of ice water into her stomach, and suddenly she was jumping away from the curtains, her hand over her mouth.

"JEEEeennnn ..." came a single voice. "JEEEeennnn ..."

Jen froze. Whose voice was it? Was it someone she knew? A stranger? Who could it be? There was only one way to find out ...

2 LISTENING

a 03.05 Listen to part of a conversation between two students at a university. Are the sentences true or false?

1 Education is the main topic of the conversation.
2 One of the speakers is a journalist.
3 One of the speakers is from Africa.
4 The speakers have not met before.
5 One speaker describes his/her family.
6 Relationships are the main topic of the conversation.
7 The conversation is an interview.
8 One speaker is a professional athlete.

b Listen to the conversation again and check (✓) the correct answers.

1 What is Ben studying in college?
 a ☐ economics
 b ☐ physics
 c ☐ political science
2 How old is Ben?
 a ☐ 24
 b ☐ 28
 c ☐ 32
3 Roxana is surprised that Ben … .
 a ☐ has a girlfriend
 b ☐ is already married
 c ☐ is not in a relationship
4 How many sisters does Ben have?
 a ☐ 3
 b ☐ 5
 c ☐ 6
5 Ben believes he is confident because … .
 a ☐ he has always been good at sports
 b ☐ his family took care of him
 c ☐ there are so many women in his family
6 Why did Ben not like Zippy when they first met?
 a ☐ Zippy did not understand Ben's sense of humor.
 b ☐ Zippy was a better soccer player than Ben.
 c ☐ Zippy's sister had an argument with Ben.

c Write a conversation between two people discussing family and friendship. Use these questions to help you:

- How would you describe your childhood?
- Do you keep in touch with friends you made in school?
- How important is it for your friends to come from the same background as you?
- What other things are important in a good friendship?

Review and extension

1 GRAMMAR

Correct the sentences.

1 He called me while I got ready to go out.
 He called me while I was getting ready to go out.
2 I use to have long hair when I was a little girl.
3 He played basketball when he fell and hurt his ankle.
4 When he got to his house, he was angry because someone broke his window.
5 I got to the train station five minutes late this morning and, unfortunately, my normal train already left.
6 After the movie, we were going to the café for coffee.
7 Did you used to play soccer when you were in school?
8 I didn't used to like English when I was in school.

2 VOCABULARY

Correct the sentences.

1 I've never had a very good relation with my sister.
 I've never had a very good relationship with my sister.
2 Joanne's mother died when she was three, so she was grown up by her grandparents.
3 I got knowing Jasmine really well when we went traveling around South America together.
4 All my relatives met together at my dad's birthday party.
5 I can't wait to hang up with my cousins at Thanksgiving.
6 She doesn't go along very well with her two brothers.
7 We have a lot on common, such as our love for literature.
8 My little brother's very calm and patient, so he looks after our mother because she's like that, too.

3 WORDPOWER *have*

Complete the sentences with the words in the box.

idea ~~accident~~ bite look time lunch

1 He had a car *accident* on his way home from work, but luckily he didn't get hurt.
2 We had a great ________ at Debbie's party.
3 I felt really hungry, so I had ________ at 12 o'clock.
4 I had no ________ they had gotten married.
5 Are those your vacation photos? Can I have a ________?
6 Let's go have a ________ after work. All those meetings made me hungry.

REVIEW YOUR PROGRESS

Look again at Review Your Progress on p. 42 of the Student's Book. How well can you do these things now?
3 = very well 2 = well 1 = not so well

I CAN …	
talk about a friendship	☐
talk about families	☐
tell a story	☐
write about someone's life.	☐

4A I COULD SING VERY WELL WHEN I WAS YOUNGER

1 GRAMMAR
Modals and phrases of ability

a Underline the correct words to complete the sentences.

1 He *wasn't able to* / *won't be able to* / <u>*hasn't been able to*</u> practice with the band since he started his new job.
2 Your sister speaks English really well. *Could you* / *Can you* / *Have you been able to* speak it as well as she does?
3 By the time he was seven, *he can* / *he could* / *he's been able to* speak four languages fluently.
4 The banks are all closed now, but don't worry; *you'll be able to* / *you could* / *you were able to* change some money tomorrow morning.
5 He missed the last bus, but fortunately, he *could* / *can* / *was able to* find a taxi to take him back to the hotel.
6 I *can't* / *couldn't* / *haven't been able to* find where your street was, so in the end I asked a police officer.
7 Before she goes abroad on vacation, she tries to learn some of the language, since she likes *being able to* / *can* / *will be able to* say a few words to the people she meets.
8 She looked everywhere in her apartment, but she *can't* / *won't be able to* / *didn't manage to* find her car keys.

b Match 1–6 with a–f to make sentences.

1 [b] Tomorrow the weather will definitely be better, so you
2 [ ] Even when he was a child, Pablo Picasso
3 [ ] I've
4 [ ] He spoke very slowly, so we
5 [ ] I'm learning Spanish because I want to
6 [ ] We looked everywhere, but in the end, we didn't

a be able to speak to my wife's family in their language.
b will be able to go to the beach.
c were able to understand him easily.
d been able to ride a bike since I was three years old.
e manage to find a hotel room.
f could draw really well.

2 VOCABULARY Ability

a Underline the correct word to complete the sentences.

1 Running 20 marathons in less than a month was an incredible *success* / <u>*achievement*</u> / *attitude*.
2 She has the *ability* / *success* / *achievement* to learn languages very quickly.
3 Jenny has a really positive attitude *at* / *toward* / *to* her studies. She works really hard.
4 I am *bright* / *confident* / *determined* to get a good grade on the exam.
5 They were one of the most *successful* / *determined* / *confident* bands of the 1960s. They sold millions of records.
6 Unfortunately, he *succeeded in* / *achieved* / *gave up* studying languages when he was 14, so his English isn't very good.

b Complete the crossword puzzle.

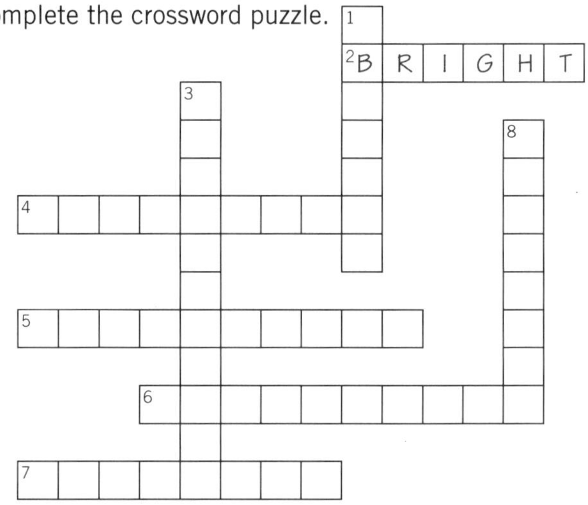

→ Across
2 She was extremely b<u>right</u>______ – probably the most intelligent student I've ever taught.
4 Rafael Nadal is an extremely c__________ tennis player – he expects to win every game he plays.
5 He was easily the most s__________ coach in the history of this basketball team. He won the championship eight times.
6 Although she felt extremely tired, she was d__________ to finish the marathon, so she continued running.
7 I prefer to work with people who have p__________ attitudes.

↓ Down
1 He had a great sense of humor, and he loved telling jokes. He always had the a__________ to make people laugh.
3 In the 1960s, NASA's greatest a__________ was landing a spacecraft on the moon.
8 Lionel Messi is probably the most t__________ soccer player of his generation.

4B ARE YOU AN INTROVERT?

1 GRAMMAR Articles

a Complete the sentences with *a*, *an*, *the*, or *Ø* (zero article).

1 On ___Ø___ Saturday, we went to ________ best Chinese restaurant in ________ Seattle.
2 Do you know if there's ________ bank near here where I can buy ________ dollars?
3 I don't go to ________ school on ________ Saturdays.
4 Sometimes it's difficult to find ________ doctor when you live in ________ country.
5 **A** I saw ________ Italian movie on TV last night. It was called *Cinema Paradiso*.
B Really? What did you think of ________ movie?
6 I think ________ Spanish people are very friendly.
7 I eat ________ fish two or three times ________ week.
8 Venice is one of ________ most beautiful cities in ________ world.

b Correct the sentences.

1 He's working as translator in U.K.
He's working as a translator in the U.K.
2 I usually go to gym three times the week.
____
3 Is there supermarket in front of bus stop near your house?
____
4 She usually goes to the school on bus.
____
5 I often listen to radio before I go to the bed.
____
6 The British pop groups are very popular in U.S.
____
7 There isn't the subway station near my hotel, so I'll have to take taxi.
____
8 Usain Bolt was fastest man in world at Olympic Games in 2016.
____

2 VOCABULARY Personality adjectives

a Complete the sentences with the words in the box.

sensitive talkative reserved shy
~~lively~~ serious outgoing sociable

1 Ana always has funny stories to tell. She's very ___lively___ and fun to be around.
2 Carla's really ________. She likes spending time with other people, and she's very good at making new friends.
3 Sam's extremely ________. You have to be very careful with what you say to him because he gets upset very easily.
4 Amanda's very ________. She doesn't like meeting new people, and she hates going to parties where she doesn't know anyone.
5 I think Marco's very ________. He has a lot of friends, and he really enjoys meeting new people.
6 My sister is so ________. She often talks to her friends on the phone for hours!
7 Gabe has very few friends and spends most of his time by himself. I think he's pretty ________.
8 James is a ________ student. He works very hard all the time, and he rarely goes out with friends.

4C EVERYDAY ENGLISH
Do you need a hand?

1 CONVERSATION SKILLS Question tags

a Match 1–9 with a–i to make questions.

1 [h] You don't eat meat anymore,
2 [ ] It's a beautiful day today,
3 [ ] Hugo's not going to ask her to marry him,
4 [ ] You haven't been waiting long for me,
5 [ ] She'd already bought him a present,
6 [ ] They'll call us when they get to the airport,
7 [ ] The twins both got good grades on their exams,
8 [ ] Andrew speaks five languages fluently,
9 [ ] You don't want any rice, Jim,

a doesn't he?
b didn't they?
c have you?
d won't they?
e isn't it?
f is he?
g hadn't she?
h do you?
i do you?

b 04.01 Listen and check.

2 USEFUL LANGUAGE Offering and asking for help

a Complete the exchanges with the words in the box.

favor need return could how
something ask ~~do~~ help hand

1 **A** Can you ___do___ something for me?
B Sure, ________ can I help you?
A Do you think you ________ cut the grass in my yard for me?
B Yes, of course. No problem.

2 **A** I have a lot of things to get ready for the party tomorrow night.
B Is there ________ I can do?
A Yes, there is, actually. Can you give me a ________ with the shopping?
B Yes, that's fine. Could I ask you a favor in ________?
A Go ahead!
B Could you lend me your black pants for tomorrow?
A No problem. I'll go get them for you.

3 **A** Could I ask you a ________, Ben?
B Of course, what do you ________?
A Could you ________ me move my desk into the other office?
B Actually, I have a bad back. Can you ________ someone else?

b 04.02 Listen and check.

3 PRONUNCIATION Intonation in question tags

a 04.03 Listen to the sentences. Does the intonation go up ↗ or down ↘? Check (✓) the correct answer.

	↗	↘
1 You've been to Cairo before, haven't you?	✓	
2 Jack's really good at tennis, isn't he?		
3 They have four children, don't they?		
4 This is the best beach in Thailand, isn't it?		
5 You're glad you left Dallas, aren't you?		
6 You didn't go to Canada last year, did you?		

4D SKILLS FOR WRITING
No experience needed

1 READING

a Read both ads and check (✓) the correct answer.

1 If you want to go on the adventure vacation in the Atlas Mountains, you … .
- a ☐ have to be good at riding camels
- b ☐ have to be under 30
- c ☐ need to have a good bike
- d ☐ shouldn't be an introvert or a shy person

2 If you want to be a volunteer English teacher, you should … .
- a ☐ have a lot of experience teaching
- b ☐ be able to work well with children
- c ☐ be able to speak another language very well
- d ☐ have your own car

VOLUNTEER ENGLISH TEACHERS NEEDED - 6 HOURS A WEEK

Duties include teaching English to schoolchildren with a low level of English in local elementary schools and to adults from all over the world who have come to work in the U.S.

No qualifications or previous teaching experience needed. Volunteers will be required to attend a training program. Candidates should be enthusiastic and outgoing and be good at working with children and adults. Candidates should have a college education, good English language skills, and some experience of learning a foreign language.

Please complete the attached online application form. One of our coordinators will get in touch with you to discuss potential opportunities. Reasonable travel expenses reimbursed.

Hiking in the Atlas Mountains

We're looking for three or four people to join us on a 2-week adventure vacation in Morocco. We're meeting up in Marrakech on April 27 and spending 10 days walking and camping in the Atlas Mountains.

We're planning to climb Mount Toubkal, the highest mountain in North Africa, visit Berber villages, and travel through a section of the Sahara Desert. We're also planning to go horseback riding and mountain biking, and we may also get the chance to ride a few camels! We'll spend the last 2–3 days exploring the fabulous city of Marrakech.

Ideally, you should be in your twenties or thirties, with an outgoing personality and a sense of adventure. You should be good at getting along well with people and making friends easily. You should be very fit and have some experience walking with a backpack in mountainous areas.

If this sounds like the trip for you, email us at the address below, and we'll get back to you as soon as possible.

Jake, Katie, and Eduardo

b Read the ads again. Are the sentences true or false?

1 There will be eight people in the group that goes on the vacation to the Atlas Mountains.
2 They're not planning to go walking in the mountains every day of the trip.
3 The people who go on this trip don't need to have any previous experience walking in mountains.
4 The adults that are learning English come from a lot of different countries.
5 New teachers don't need to receive any training.
6 It is better if new teachers have previously studied another language.

2 WRITING SKILLS
The language of ads

a Match sentences 1–8 with the reduced expressions a–h.

1 [g] Candidates don't need to pay for a place to stay.
2 ☐ Candidates must be able to drive a car.
3 ☐ We will need to see your references from your previous jobs.
4 ☐ We're looking for someone with a college degree.
5 ☐ It doesn't matter if you've never done this job before.
6 ☐ The candidate needs to have previous classroom experience.
7 ☐ Candidates should be able to speak French.
8 ☐ We will train the successful applicant to do the job.

a No previous experience needed.
b College graduate preferred.
c Teaching experience required.
d Full training program provided.
e French speaker preferred.
f Good references required.
g Accommodation provided.
h Driver's license required.

3 WRITING

a Read the notes. Write an ad for summer camp coaches.

Notes for summer camp coaches ad

Camp for children 5–12 years old

Duties: Organize indoor/outdoor activities. Get kids ready in morning. Help at meal & bed times. Entertain during free time.

Person requirements: Energetic, enthusiastic, sense of adventure, sense of humor, & positive attitude. Good at sports & art, etc. Must love working with children & work well with others on a team. 18 or over. College students/graduates preferred.

No experience required. Two-day training course.

Online application form & résumé to Human Resources Dept. HR will contact applicants for interviews.

UNIT 4
Reading and listening extension

1 READING

a Read the text and check (✓) the correct answers.

1 Where might you usually see this kind of text?
- a ☐ in a newspaper
- b ☐ in an email from a friend
- c ☐ on the back of a book

2 According to the reviewer, self-help books … .
- a ☐ are usually very expensive
- b ☐ have a large number of readers
- c ☐ help readers earn more money

3 Where did Burkeman go to collect information for the book?
- a ☐ capital cities in Europe
- b ☐ countries in North and South America
- c ☐ many different places

4 The reviewer enjoys a description of … .
- a ☐ a family party
- b ☐ a funeral in a small town
- c ☐ a traditional festival

b Read the text again. Are the sentences true or false?

1 The phrase "worth their weight in gold" in the first paragraph means "valuable."
2 *The Antidote* is a typical example of a self-help book.
3 Burkeman did not expect to find happiness in some of the places he visited.
4 Burkeman discovers that life is more difficult for people when they have a lot of money.
5 Burkeman says we cannot understand happiness unless we also have bad experiences.
6 People are often happy during the Day of the Dead.
7 Although there are some good parts, the reviewer does not recommend this book.

c Write a review of a non-fiction book you have enjoyed reading. Include the following:

- the name of the author and the title of the book
- a paragraph describing the general topic of the book
- a paragraph describing the main ideas in the book
- a paragraph describing the best part(s) of the book
- an explanation of why other people should read the book.

BOOK **REVIEWS**

THE ANTIDOTE: HAPPINESS FOR PEOPLE WHO CAN'T STAND POSITIVE THINKING by Oliver Burkeman

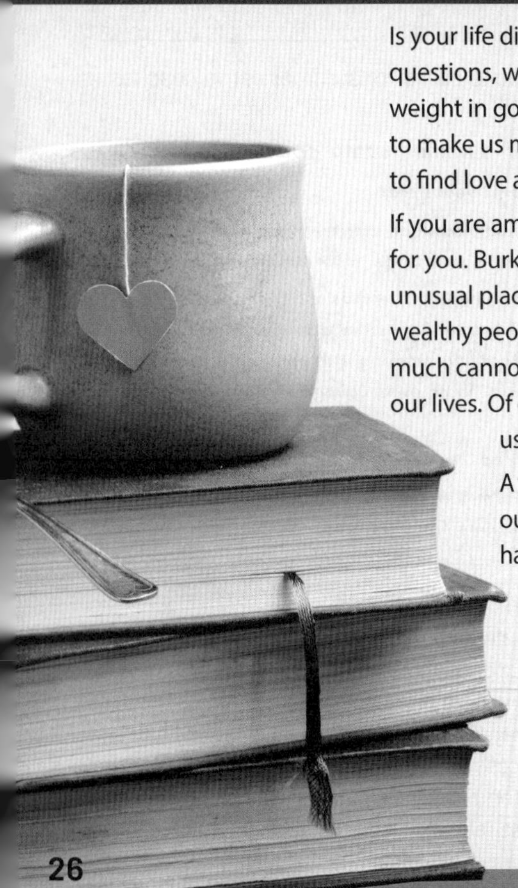

Is your life disappointing? Does that make you feel depressed? If you answered yes to those two questions, what can you do to find happiness? The answers to these questions can be worth their weight in gold – last year, people spent almost $11 billion on self-help books. These books promise to make us more confident, more sociable, and more successful. They tell us that all we really need to find love and achieve our goals is a positive attitude.

If you are amused by promises like these, then Oliver Burkeman's book *The Antidote* might just be for you. Burkeman has traveled the world in search of happiness, and he has found it in some very unusual places. For example, he meets poor people in Africa who seem to be happier than some wealthy people he knows in London. For Burkeman, this shows us that people who do not own very much cannot worry about losing it. In other words, having a lot of things can add a lot of stress to our lives. Of course, he is not saying that poor people in Africa have an easy life. Instead, Burkeman uses this example to talk about "negative paths."

A "negative path" is important for a satisfying life. He suggests that we need to remind ourselves that bad things happen and that we should learn to live with them. True happiness – if it exists – must include both positive and negative experiences. A complete life should be one that knows hate as well as love and illness as well as health.

In my favorite part of the book, Burkeman takes us to a small village in Mexico on the Day of the Dead. The Day of the Dead is a festival that celebrates everyone who has died. However, it is not a sad festival at all, but a lively party for friends and family. According to Burkeman, we need events like this to remember why we should be happy more often. *The Antidote* is an interesting book that has the ability to make you feel that happiness really is possible.

2 LISTENING

a 04.04 Listen to an expert in advertising tell a story during a talk to college students and check (✓) the correct answers.

1 Where did the story take place?
a ☐ in England b ☐ in Germany c ☐ in Russia

2 Why did Frederick want people to start eating potatoes?
a ☐ They were cheap and easy to grow.
b ☐ They were the solution to a problem.
c ☐ They were very popular with the people.

3 Frederick was surprised that the people … .
a ☐ did not know how to grow potatoes
b ☐ gave the potatoes to their animals
c ☐ said they could not eat the potatoes

4 According to the speaker, the story can teach us something about … .
a ☐ food b ☐ history c ☐ psychology

b Listen again and correct the information in the sentences. Use the words in the box to help you. You do not need all the words.

animal be successful bread business hungry meat psychology soldier steal ~~talented~~

1 Frederick II is sometimes called Frederick the Great because he was so tall.
Frederick II is sometimes called Frederick the Great because he was so talented.

2 Cheese was the most important part of most people's diet.
____

3 Frederick thought that if people had potatoes, they would not be angry anymore.
____

4 People in Kolberg said their children could not eat potatoes.
____

5 People understood that potatoes were valuable when they saw the gates around Frederick's garden.
____

6 People began eating potatoes from Frederick's garden.
____

7 Frederick's plan did not work.
____

8 Frederick's plan was an example of good farming.
____

c Think of a story about a famous person or event in your country. Use these questions to make notes:

- Does the story teach a lesson?
(For example, can the story help people become more patient / more confident / healthier?)
- Who are the main characters in the story?
- What happens?

Write the story.

Review and extension

1 GRAMMAR

Correct the sentences.

1 I've could speak English since I was seven years old.
I've been able to speak English since I was seven years old.
2 When she goes to movies, she doesn't like seeing the horror movies.
3 Will you can help me with my math homework tonight?
4 I love watching the documentaries about the whales.
5 She would like to can play the piano as well as her sister.
6 He usually gets to the work at about 8:30 in summer.
7 We weren't able find the restaurant, so we went to the pizzeria instead.
8 It's one of best shopping websites on Internet.

2 VOCABULARY

Correct the sentences.

1 He has very positive attitude toward his studies.
He has a very positive attitude toward his studies.
2 People really like Victor's sociabel personality.
3 The Internet is surely one of man's greatest abilities of the last century.
4 My uncle was a very succesful businessman in the 1960s.
5 Sandra is very inteligent. Did you know she can speak four languages?
6 José is so talkative sometimes – he stands in the corner at parties and doesn't talk to anyone.

3 WORDPOWER *so* and *such*

Complete the sentences with the words in the box.

so far such ~~such a~~ and so on so tired or so

1 He's *such a* talented musician!
2 He's been fishing for six hours, and ________, he hasn't caught any fish.
3 It's a short book – no more than 100 pages ________.
4 To make a cake, you'll need all the usual things – sugar, flour, butter, ________.
5 We didn't expect ________ rainy weather this weekend.
6 I was ________ that I fell asleep on the bus.

REVIEW YOUR PROGRESS

Look again at Review Your Progress on p. 54 of the Student's Book. How well can you do these things now?
3 = very well 2 = well 1 = not so well

I CAN …	
describe people and their abilities	☐
describe feelings	☐
offer and ask for help	☐
write an informal online ad.	☐

5A PEOPLE WILL CARE MORE ABOUT THE ENVIRONMENT

1 GRAMMAR Future forms

a Match 1–8 with a–h to make sentences and questions.

1 [f] Jack really hates his job, so he's going to
2 [ ] Don't worry – this year I promise I won't
3 [ ] At 1 o'clock, I'm
4 [ ] Brian's been studying very hard, so I'm sure he
5 [ ] I probably won't
6 [ ] What a beautiful day! Should we
7 [ ] Look at those dark clouds. I think it's
8 [ ] Your train doesn't get here until 11:30, so should I

a meeting Laura for lunch at *Café Classic*.
b 'll get good grades on his exams.
c meet you at the station in my car?
d going to rain. Let's stay inside.
e go to the beach this afternoon?
f start looking for a new one in September.
g forget your birthday!
h see her today, since she usually visits her grandparents on Sundays.

b Correct the sentences.

1 **A** Will we go out for pizza tonight?
Should we go out for pizza tonight?
B Yes, good idea. I'm calling the pizzeria to book a table.
____

2 **A** What time might your brother arrive?
____
B This evening. I drive to the train station to meet him at 6:30.
____

3 Hello, John. The traffic's really bad downtown. We're being about 20 minutes late.
____

4 In my opinion, the next president of the U.S. can be a woman.
____

5 Will I help you bring in the groceries from the car?
____

6 **A** What time will you have your hair cut this afternoon?
____
B I've made an appointment for 3 o'clock.

7 I don't think Brazil is winning the soccer game tomorrow.
____

8 **A** What are Eric's plans for the future?
B I don't know. Perhaps he's getting a job at that new hotel at the beach.
____

2 VOCABULARY Environmental issues

a Match 1–5 with a–e to make sentences.

1 [a] People should be able to recycle
2 [ ] Air pollution has seriously damaged
3 [ ] The environmental group is trying to prevent
4 [ ] Around 1,500 pandas survive
5 [ ] Environmental organizations are trying to save

a more than 50% of their household trash.
b the Siberian tiger from extinction.
c in the mountains of Western China.
d the destruction of the rainforest in Puerto Rico.
e the outside of the pyramids near Cairo.

b Complete the sentences with the words in the box.

wildlife conservation environmentally pollution climate destroyed ~~environment~~ endangered

1 We have to protect the *environment* for future generations.
2 Scientists are very worried about ________ change.
3 The ________ caused by cars and trucks is affecting air quality downtown.
4 The hybrid car is the most ________ friendly car.
5 Large areas of the Amazon rainforest are ________ by farmers every year.
6 The black rhino is an ________ species. There are very few animals left in the wild.
7 There is incredible ________ in Kenya, including lions, elephants, and giraffes.
8 I'm working on a ________ project right now to protect and preserve rare plants.

3 PRONUNCIATION Sound and spelling: *a*

a How is the underlined letter *a* pronounced in each word in the box? Complete the chart with the words.

plant abroad save along dam danger nature local gorilla mammal education after animal branch charity

/eɪ/ (e.g., *paper*)	/æ/ (e.g., *and*)	/ə/ (e.g., *climate*)

b 05.01 Listen and check.

5B IF NATURE CAN DO IT, WE CAN COPY IT

1 GRAMMAR Present and future real conditionals

a Put the words in the correct order to make sentences.

1 going / offer me / to London / I'm / the job, / if / move / they / to .
If they offer me the job, I'm going to move to London.

2 when / at / plane / we'll / JFK Airport / call / lands / our / you .

____

3 tigers, / if / extinct / we / they'll / stop hunting / don't / 20 years / be / in .

____

4 too / the / when / cold, / south / birds / gets / weather / fly / the .

____

5 new laptop / my / a / help him / I / the house / dad / buy me / if / paint / will .

____

6 or an / you / later, / apple / if / feel hungry / have / a banana .

____

7 11 o'clock / the / be there / with / train / problem / unless / at / a / I'll / there's .

____

8 take / the / soon, / a / I'm / unless / going to / comes / taxi / bus .

____

b 05.02 Listen and check.

c Underline the correct words to complete the sentences.

1 If they *win* / *will win* / *are winning* the game tomorrow, *they're* / *they'll be* / *they were* the champions.
2 If you *will see* / *see* / *don't see* Kate tomorrow, *invite* / *you'll invite* / *you're going to invite* her to the party.
3 When the chameleon *will go* / *goes* / *is going to go* into a different environment, its skin *will change* / *is going to change* / *changes* color.
4 *Unless* / *If* / *When* it stops raining soon, we *couldn't* / *can't* / *won't be able to* go to the park this afternoon.
5 *You will open* / *Open* / *You're going to open* the window if you *feel* / *will feel* / *don't feel* too hot.
6 If *she's going to miss* / *she'll miss* / *she misses* her flight this evening, she *had to* / *will have to* / *has to* come tomorrow instead.
7 When the sun *will go* / *goes* / *is going to go* behind the clouds, it *usually feels* / *will usually feel* / *usually felt* much colder.
8 He *can't* / *won't be able to* / *couldn't* find your apartment unless you *will send* / *are going to send* / *send* him directions.

2 VOCABULARY The natural world

a Look at the plants and animals and label the pictures. Use the words in the box.

petals	scales	paw	tail	branches
web	fur	~~skin~~	feathers	

1 *skin*

2 _______________

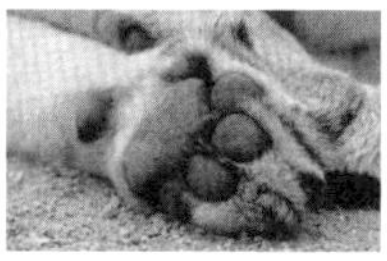

3 _______________

4 _______________

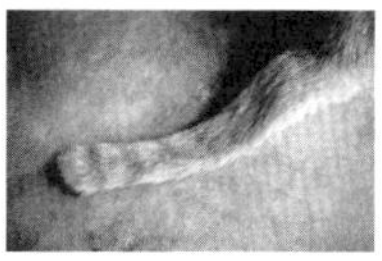

5 _______________

6 _______________

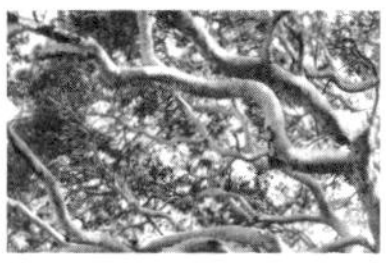

7 _______________

8 _______________

9 _______________

b Complete the crossword puzzle.

→ Across

1 One of the most famous *national* *parks* in the U.S. is Yosemite in California.
4 There are five _______________ in the world: the Pacific, the Atlantic, the Indian, the Arctic, and the Southern.
6 The largest _______________ in Africa is the Sahara.
7 The Nile is the longest _______________ in the world.
9 The highest _______________ in the world are the Angel Falls in Venezuela.

↓ Down

2 Large areas of the Amazon _______________ are destroyed every year.
3 The largest _______________ in the world is Superior, on the border between Canada and the U.S.
5 _______________ are usually much smaller than rivers.
8 In 1940, four French teenagers discovered prehistoric paintings in an underground _______________ in Lascaux in the southwest of France.

5C EVERYDAY ENGLISH

Why did you decide to open your own business?

1 USEFUL LANGUAGE
Reasons, results, and examples

a Complete the sentences with the words in the box.

like as a result due to because of for instance ~~because~~ such as since so

1 Alicia doesn't enjoy her current job ___because___ she often has to work until 8 p.m.
2 There are a lot of things I can offer this company, ___________ my talent for creating attractive websites and my experience in management.
3 It took me over an hour to get to work this morning ___________ a serious accident on the highway.
4 **A** There are some things I don't like about my job.
B ___________?
A Well, ___________, I don't like having to drive 50 kilometers to work every day.
5 Tom didn't get along with his new boss, ___________ he decided to apply for a job at another company.
6 ___________ there weren't any meeting rooms free at 11 o'clock, they had to hold the meeting in his office.
7 I had to stay late at work yesterday. ___________, I didn't get home until 9 o'clock.
8 My train arrived 45 minutes late this morning ___________ the bad weather in Chicago.

b 05.03 Listen and check.

2 CONVERSATION SKILLS
Giving yourself time to think

a Complete the sentences with the words in the box.

second well sure ~~see~~ question

1 **A** So how old is your father now?
B Let me ___see___. I think he'll be 62 in June.
2 **A** So what skills can you bring to this job?
B ___________, to begin with, I have excellent project management skills.
3 **A** So why do you want to leave your current job?
B That's a good ___________. The main reason is that I need a new challenge.
4 **A** What time does their plane arrive at Heathrow Airport?
B Just a ___________. I'll check their email.

b 05.04 Listen and check.

3 PRONUNCIATION
Voiced and unvoiced consonants

a 05.05 Listen to the pairs of words. Check (✓) the words you hear.

1 ☐ pour ☑ bore
2 ☐ pear ☐ bear
3 ☐ cap ☐ cab
4 ☐ plume ☐ bloom
5 ☐ cup ☐ cub

5D SKILLS FOR WRITING

Taking care of our oceans

1 READING

a Read the essay and underline the correct phrases to complete the text.

b Read the essay again and check (✓) the correct answer.

In the writer's opinion, ...

a ☐ gas cars are more efficient than electric cars
b ☐ diesel cars are more environmentally friendly than electric cars
c ☐ electric cars are better now than a few years ago
d ☐ people should buy gas cars in the future

c Are the sentences true or false?

1 Electric cars are more expensive now than they were a few years ago.
2 Electric cars do not cause problems for the air we breathe.
3 Some people become stressed due to the noise caused by traffic.
4 It costs the same to operate electric cars and gas cars.
5 It is more convenient to recharge an electric car at home than to drive to a gas station.

Electric cars are the future

If you are thinking of buying a new car soon, perhaps you should consider getting an electric car. In the last few years, electric cars have become more efficient, and they're now much cheaper to buy. So why should we switch to electric cars?

[1]*In conclusion / First of all / Finally*, air pollution in our cities has become a serious problem over the past 50 years or so. Electric cars do not produce any CO_2 emissions, and as a result, they don't pollute the atmosphere. If we drive electric cars, this will significantly improve the quality of the air we breathe.

[2]*Firstly / Finally / Secondly*, electric cars are quieter than cars that use gas or diesel. Today's cars and trucks cause a lot of noise pollution, and this can make people feel very stressed.

[3]*Secondly / Finally / First of all*, they are cheaper to operate than conventional cars. The price of gas is extremely high, and the cost per kilometer of an electric car is much lower than a regular gas or diesel car. In addition, it is more convenient to recharge your electric car at home than to drive to a gas station to fill up your tank.

[4]*In conclusion / First of all / In addition*, I would say that if we really care about the environment, we should all consider buying electric cars. They have improved a great deal in recent years, and they will definitely be the vehicle of the future.

2 WRITING

a Read the notes. Write an essay about the advantages of solar panels.

Notes for essay about solar panels

Spend too much on electricity? Solar panels may be the solution.

1) Efficient and good for environment. No pollution, e.g., no carbon dioxide or other gases. If plenty of sunshine, can generate all electricity for the home.

2) Not cheap to buy, but will save money on electricity bills in long term & energy companies buy extra electricity produced. Result: may actually make money.

3) Can increase value of house. People pay higher price to save money on electricity.

4) Conclusion. A good idea. Environmentally friendly & cheap electricity.

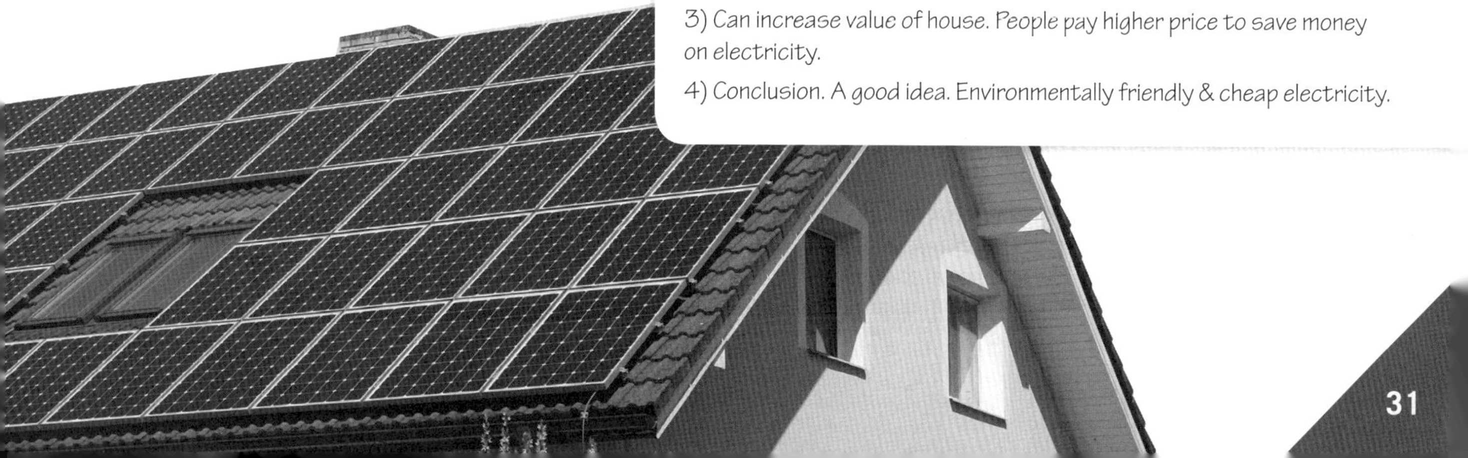

UNIT 5

Reading and listening extension

1 READING

a Read the student's essay. Match paragraphs A–D with functions 1–6. There are two extra functions you do not need.

☐ Paragraph A ☐ Paragraph C
☐ Paragraph B ☐ Paragraph D

1 to describe the consequences of climate change
2 to describe weather problems
3 to give the student's own opinion
4 to introduce the main topic and explain the purpose of the essay
5 to describe why the main argument of climate change deniers is false
6 to describe who the climate change deniers and defenders are

b Read the essay again and check (✓) the correct answer.

1 According to environmental scientists, … .
  a ☐ forest fires and snow have changed the world's climate
  b ☐ humans have caused climate change
  c ☐ it is not possible to protect the environment from climate change

2 The writer explains that the purpose of the essay is … .
  a ☐ to explain who climate change deniers are and explain the problems with their main argument
  b ☐ to prove that climate change does not really exist
  c ☐ to prove that environmental scientists are telling the truth

3 Why is the Industrial Revolution important to studying the climate?
  a ☐ The weather changed unexpectedly when it began.
  b ☐ Scientists believe it's what started the increase in global temperatures.
  c ☐ It gave scientists new inventions to study the climate that they never had before.

4 The writer's main purpose in paragraph B is to … .
  a ☐ show why some people might not believe in climate change
  b ☐ explain why climate change deniers' main argument isn't correct
  c ☐ describe changes in climate patterns over the last 700 years

5 Why does the writer mention that 97% of scientists believe that smoking causes cancer?
  a ☐ to illustrate that smoking pollutes the environment
  b ☐ to show that businesspeople who smoke are the same ones who deny climate change
  c ☐ to show that the same amount of scientists believe in the connection between smoking and cancer as they do between humans and climate change

6 The writer's main purpose in paragraph C is to show … .
  a ☐ how the business interests of many climate change deniers influence their opinions
  b ☐ why climate change deniers are wrong
  c ☐ why climate scientists are right

7 According to the writer, … .
  a ☐ it is not too late to save the planet
  b ☐ terrible weather proves that climate change exists
  c ☐ we should not trust environmental scientists

"It will be a long time before we know the true effects of climate change and all the harm we are causing to our planet." Discuss.

A All around the world, we hear stories of terrible weather becoming even worse. For instance, while forests in Australia and California are on fire, fields in Egypt are covered in snow, and cities across Europe and Asia are under water. Most people know that these events are connected to climate change. Scientists say that if we cannot protect our environment, we will destroy the planet and everyone and everything on it. Despite this, some people, known as climate change deniers, still say there is no such thing as climate change. In this essay, I will explain the problems with climate change deniers' arguments, and I will look at both the main believers and deniers of climate change.

B First of all, climate change deniers say that the rise in temperatures is just part of Earth's natural cycle. For example, they talk about two periods in history known as the Little Ice Age, from the year 1300 to 1850, and the Medieval Warm Period, from 900 to 1300. These were two periods in history when temperatures became colder and warmer than usual. However, the Little Ice Age and the Medieval Warm Period were just changes in certain areas, not all over the world. A study of the last 2,000 years shows that the only time temperatures have increased all around the world has been in the last 150 years, since the Industrial Revolution started. In fact, more than 98% of the planet has warmed in the last 150 years. Therefore, this warming is not part of a natural cycle. It is something caused by humans that we have never seen before.

C It is also important to look at who accepts and who denies climate change. More than 97% of climate scientists believe in climate change and that humans are causing it. Similarly, 97% of scientists agree that smoking causes cancer. Nowadays, almost everyone agrees that smoking causes cancer. If nobody denies that anymore, then why should we deny that humans are causing climate change? We also need to look at who the main deniers are. Most of them are businesspeople who depend on oil and natural gases, the main causes of climate change, to make money. If they accept the truth about climate change, then they have to accept that their businesses are part of the problem and make big changes.

D In conclusion, we cannot believe climate change deniers because their main argument is not correct and because many are only protecting their business interests. We must believe climate scientists and stop the horrible effects of climate change before it is too late.

c Write an essay. Read the statement below. Then use the Internet to find ideas, facts, and information that agree and disagree with the statement. Decide whether you agree or disagree with the statement.

> **"In the future, people will fight over access to water, not oil." Discuss.**

2 LISTENING

a 05.06 Listen to the introduction to a lecture. Then put these parts of the introduction in the correct order.

- [ ] He describes a result of not taking care of the environment.
- [ ] He explains how the talk will be organized.
- [ ] He explains why local problems are important.
- [ ] He gives the title of his talk.
- [1] He uses a story to explain a main idea of the lecture.

b Listen again. Are the sentences true or false?

1 The writer Theodore Dalrymple sees many different kinds of trash in the streets.
2 The lecturer says that people need to understand that the environment includes towns and cities.
3 The lecturer says people need to save the environment before they make their streets clean and organized.
4 The lecturer explains that we need to invent more environmentally friendly methods of clearing up trash.
5 The talk will include a description of how we can change people's ideas.
6 The lecturer believes that people must make small changes before they can make bigger ones.

c Write a letter to a newspaper about a problem with your local environment. For example:

There's too much trash in the local parks.

Include each of these in your letter:

- the consequences of not doing anything about the problem
- solutions to the problem
- why some people may disagree with your ideas
- what you say to the people who disagree with your solution.

Review and extension

1 GRAMMAR

Correct the sentences.

1 What time will we meet outside the movie theater?
What time should we meet outside the movie theater?
2 If he'll arrive before 2:00, we'll take him to that Italian restaurant for lunch.
3 Wait! I help you go shopping if you like.
4 Unless it will rain this afternoon, we play golf.
5 I can't come with you because I will play basketball with Pablo this afternoon. We meet at the park at 3:00.
6 When they will win the next game, they'll win the gold medal.

2 VOCABULARY

Correct the sentences.

1 We must do everything we can to protect the nature.
We must do everything we can to protect the environment.
2 There are fantastic beaches on the cost near Rio de Janeiro.
3 It hardly ever rains in the dessert.
4 Air dirt is a serious problem in big cities like Tokyo.
5 The leafs of that tree are as big as my hand.
6 She's working on a very important project to safe endangered species from extinction.

3 WORDPOWER *problem*

Complete the sentences with the words in the box. You might need to change the verb form.

cause	tackle	be aware of	face	fix	~~solve~~

1 The IT department *solved* the problem with my computer immediately.
2 I'm sure the mechanic will ________ your car.
3 Sometimes it ________ problems on your computer if you install a new program while other programs are open.
4 The government has just launched a new campaign to try to ________ obesity among teenagers.
5 These days, most people ________ the problem of deforestation in the Amazon rainforest.
6 My baseball team is ________ a big problem after losing their last five games.

REVIEW YOUR PROGRESS

Look again at Review Your Progress on p. 66 of the Student's Book. How well can you do these things now?
3 = very well 2 = well 1 = not so well

I CAN ...	
talk about the future	☐
talk about *if* and *when*	☐
give reasons, results, and examples	☐
write a discussion essay.	☐

6A YOU SHOULD WEAR GOOD WALKING SHOES

1 GRAMMAR Modals of obligation

a Underline the correct words to complete the conversation.

PAUL I have my English exam tomorrow morning.
MOM That's right. So what time do you [1] *should / have to / must* be at school?
PAUL Well, the exam starts at 9 o'clock, so I [2] *can't / don't have to / can* be late.
MOM I think you [3] *shouldn't / must not / ought to* leave earlier than usual, in case there's a lot of traffic.
PAUL Yes, that's a good idea.
MOM And what are you going to do after the exam?
PAUL Well, I [4] *must not / shouldn't / don't have to* stay at school in the afternoon, so I [5] *can / should / must* come home for lunch.
MOM Good, just two more things. It says on this information sheet that students [6] *can / must / shouldn't* show their ID cards before the exam.
PAUL Don't worry. I always take my ID card with me to school.
MOM It also says you [7] *don't have to / must / can't* use a dictionary during the exam, so don't take one with you.
PAUL Yes, I know. I'll leave it at home.
MOM OK, good. By the way, it's 10 o'clock. You [8] *shouldn't / have to / must* go to bed late tonight.
PAUL No, you're right. I'll go to bed now.
MOM OK, good night. And good luck tomorrow!

b 06.01 Listen and check.

c Match 1–6 with a–f to make sentences.

1 [f] The service was terrible, so you shouldn't
2 [ ] Slow down! We're near a school, so you can't
3 [ ] In my experience, you don't usually have to
4 [ ] I'm worried about renting a car in Ecuador. I think we should
5 [ ] It's all right here. The sign says you can
6 [ ] It's Mom's birthday tomorrow. You have to

a take off your shoes when you go into someone's house in the U.S.
b drive so fast.
c buy her a present this afternoon.
d park your car here after 6:30 p.m.
e read about the rules for driving in the guidebook before we decide.
f leave the server a big tip.

2 VOCABULARY Compound nouns

a Match 1–8 with a–h to make sentences.

1 [c] When I go on long walks in the forest, I always take insect
2 [ ] Don't forget to pack your walking
3 [ ] She bought a new backpack
4 [ ] I'm going to buy that coffee cup for my mom at the souvenir
5 [ ] Should we check the guidebook about the city's different neighborhoods
6 [ ] We were given some great insights by the tour
7 [ ] You should put on some sunscreen
8 [ ] Jack loves history and has lived in this city his whole life, so he'd be a great tour

a before we book a hotel?
b store. She'll love it.
c repellent. I don't want anything to bite me!
d shoes, or else your feet are going to hurt.
e guide into the Mexican culture that made our city tour much more interesting.
f because her old one was too small.
g guide. He's really friendly, too.
h because we're going to be outside all day.

3 PRONUNCIATION Word stress: compound nouns

a 06.02 Listen to the compound nouns and underline the stressed word.

1 guidebook
2 insect repellent
3 walking shoes
4 backpack
5 tour guide
6 culture shock

6B IT'S TASTIER THAN I EXPECTED

1 GRAMMAR Comparatives and superlatives

a Put the words in the correct order to make sentences.

1 wasn't / as / my / nearly / I / good / as / lunch / expected .
My lunch wasn't nearly as good as I expected.

2 by far / is / luxurious / the / most / I've / hotel / stayed in / this / ever .

3 than / tennis / much / I do / plays / she / better .

4 nearly / today's / hot / as / was / as / not / yesterday / it .

5 most / these / are / ever / shoes / expensive / I've / the / bought .

6 cheaper / go to / the restaurant / we / far / usually / this restaurant / is / than .

7 hardest / that was / the / I've / my / in / exam / taken / life .

8 got / last / than / usual / earlier / home / she / night .

b 06.03 Listen and check.

c Correct <u>two</u> mistakes in each sentence.

1 He speaks quicklier that I do.
He speaks more quickly than I do.

2 San Francisco is many expensiver than Chicago.

3 They make the better pizzas of Rome.

4 Colin is more smart that his brother.

5 That was the most sad movie I ever seen.

6 The exam wasn't near as hard that I expected.

7 I think this is most simple recipe in the book.

8 Right now, the weather in Turkey is a little more warm that in Spain.

d 06.04 Listen and check.

2 VOCABULARY Describing food

a <u>Underline</u> the correct words to complete the sentences.

1 This coffee is too *sour / bitter / <u>sweet</u>*. I don't usually add sugar.

2 To serve spaghetti, add the sauce to the *creamy / heavy / cooked* pasta, then top with parmesan cheese.

3 When you make a salad, it's better to use *cooked / raw / sour* carrots so they don't lose their vitamins.

4 Sorry, I can't eat this cereal quietly. It's really *crunchy / sour / raw*.

5 It's the butter and milk in this sauce that makes it taste so *crunchy / creamy / sour*.

6 This yogurt's horrible. It tastes really *dried / heavy / sour*. When did you buy it?

7 It's always better to use *fresh / sweet / heavy* herbs when you're cooking. They taste much better.

8 I had a really *light / raw / heavy* dinner last night, so I didn't sleep very well.

b Complete the sentences with the words in the box.

add	stir	mix	mash	chop
fry	~~squeeze~~	serve	heat up	

1 You need to squeeze the juice from four large oranges to make a glass of orange juice.

2 When the potatoes are cooked, take them out of the water, then ________ them with a little butter and milk until they are smooth and creamy.

3 Using a sharp knife, ________ the onions and peppers finely, then ________ them in a little olive oil for about five minutes.

4 ________ a little salt and pepper to the tomato sauce, and cook it slowly for about twenty minutes.

5 To make the salad, ________ the lettuce, tomatoes, onions, and cucumber together, put a little olive oil and balsamic vinegar on top, and ________ with some fresh bread and butter.

6 ________ the mixture of milk, butter, and flour in a saucepan, and ________ continuously with a wooden spoon to ensure a smooth, creamy sauce.

6C EVERYDAY ENGLISH
Well, what would you recommend?

1 USEFUL LANGUAGE Asking for and giving recommendations

a Complete the conversation with the words in the box.

worth should ~~think~~ wrong kidding were
better recommend would definitely

A So where do you [1] ___think___ I should take my mother on vacation?
B If I [2] __________ you, I'd take her somewhere warm, like Italy.
A You've been to Italy lots of times, haven't you? Well, what would you [3] __________ ?
B Well, you should [4] __________ go to Rome – it's such a beautiful city.
A That's a good idea. And when [5] __________ you go?
B Hmm, let me see. Well, you can't go [6] __________ in May or June when it's not that hot. It's much [7] __________ to go then than in July or August. Those months are too hot to go sightseeing.
A And where do you think we [8] __________ stay in Rome?
B Well, there are some wonderful hotels downtown, but they're at least $200 a night.
A You're [9] __________! I had no idea it would be that expensive. I can't afford to pay that much!
B Oh, well, in that case, it's probably [10] __________ finding a hotel outside downtown, then.
A Yes, that makes sense. Thanks for your advice.

b 06.05 Listen and check.

c Underline the correct words to complete the sentences.

1 You should definitely *to visit* / *visiting* / *visit* the British Museum when you're in London.
2 What dress would you *wearing* / *wear* / *to wear* to the party?
3 It's much better *take* / *to take* / *taking* the train from Amsterdam to Paris.
4 It's probably worth *book* / *booking* / *to book* a hotel before you go.
5 If I were you, *I'll* / *I did* / *I'd* take the job in Portland.
6 Do you think I *would* / *should* / *to* buy this watch?

d 06.06 Listen and check.

2 PRONUNCIATION Sounding interested

a 06.07 Listen to the exchanges. Does Speaker B sound excited or bored? Check (✓) the correct box.

1 **A** My boyfriend's taking me to Paris this weekend!
B Wow! That's amazing. excited ☑ bored ☐
2 **A** I've been accepted to Harvard University!
B Oh, really? That's good. excited ☐ bored ☐
3 **A** I got the best exam grades in my class!
B That's amazing! Well done! excited ☐ bored ☐
4 **A** My dad's going to buy me a rabbit!
B Wow! That's great. excited ☐ bored ☐
5 **A** I got a promotion at work!
B Great! I'm so happy for you. excited ☐ bored ☐
6 **A** We leave for vacation on Saturday!
B I know. I can't wait! excited ☐ bored ☐

6D SKILLS FOR WRITING

It's definitely worth a visit

"The tastiest Italian food in St. Louis?" **Review A**

I took my Italian friend here for his birthday, and he absolutely loved it. The atmosphere was really relaxing, and the servers were friendly and extremely helpful. All the food was really fresh, and the portions were generous. The tiramisu that we had for our dessert was absolutely delicious. Paolo says it's the best he's ever had – apart from his mom's, of course! Although our dinner was fairly expensive, we didn't mind paying a little more than usual because the food was so good. I'd definitely recommend this restaurant if you want to eat fantastic food in a relaxing atmosphere. EMMA T

"Not the most relaxing evening ..." **Review B**

A coworker recommended this place, but we thought it was a little disappointing. First of all, the atmosphere wasn't very relaxing. It was a little noisy, perhaps because it was a Friday night and the restaurant was fairly busy. Also, the music was too loud, so it was hard to talk. Secondly, although the servers were very friendly, there weren't enough of them when we were there and so the service was slow. Unfortunately, when our food eventually arrived, it wasn't very good. Our steaks were a little overcooked, and the salad wasn't very fresh. Finally, the portions weren't very big, and we thought the meal was slightly overpriced. All in all, I'm afraid I wouldn't recommend it. DAVID M

1 READING

a Read the reviews and check (✓) the correct column.

	Review A	Review B
1 The reviewer really enjoyed the meal.		
2 The service wasn't very good.		
3 The quality of the food was good.		
4 The review of the restaurant is positive.		

b Read the reviews again. Are the sentences true or false?

1 In Emma's opinion, the service was good.
2 Emma didn't enjoy her dessert.
3 Emma thought the price of her meal was too high.
4 There weren't many people there when David went to this restaurant.
5 David had to wait a long time for his food to arrive.
6 David was a little disappointed by the quality of his food.

2 WRITING SKILLS Positive and negative language; Adverbs

a Underline the correct words to complete the sentences with a "strong" or a "weak" adverb, following the instruction in parentheses.

1 The chocolate cake was *fairly* / *absolutely* delicious. (strong)
2 Unfortunately, all the vegetables were *slightly* / *completely* overcooked. (weak)
3 The food in that new restaurant was *extremely* / *a little* boring. (weak)
4 I thought the portions were *absolutely tiny* / *fairly small*. (weak)
5 That new café is *extremely* / *fairly* expensive. (strong)
6 I thought the tomato soup was *a little* / *completely* tasteless. (strong)
7 The staff in the hotel was *reasonably* / *really* friendly. (weak)
8 When we were there, the service was *fairly* / *extremely* slow. (strong)

3 WRITING

a Write two reviews, one for each of the restaurants in the fact files below. One review should be mostly positive, the other mostly negative.

RESTAURANT FACT FILE

NAME:	***Chez Pierre***
LOCATION:	downtown
TYPE OF FOOD:	French, e.g., meat (steak, lamb, etc.), fish / seafood, salads
QUALITY OF FOOD:	
ATMOSPHERE:	
MUSIC:	
TYPE OF CUSTOMER:	businesspeople, romantic couples
SERVICE/ATTITUDE OF SERVERS:	
PRICE:	$$$$
VALUE FOR MONEY:	
WHEN BUSY:	weekday lunchtimes, weekends

RESTAURANT FACT FILE

NAME:	***Villa Borghese***
LOCATION:	at the beach
TYPE OF FOOD:	Italian, e.g., pizza, pasta, risotto, fish, meat, ice cream
QUALITY OF FOOD:	
ATMOSPHERE:	
MUSIC:	
TYPE OF CUSTOMER:	families and groups of young people
SERVICE/ATTITUDE OF SERVERS:	
PRICE:	$
VALUE FOR MONEY:	
WHEN BUSY:	every evening

Reading and listening extension

1 READING

a Read the text. Are the sentences true or false?

1 This text is a newspaper article.
2 The writer's name is Alex Walker.
3 The writer says that she enjoyed her first visit to the city despite one or two problems.
4 The writer says that the city has improved.

b Read the text again and check (✓) the correct answers.

1 How long has Alex Walker been mayor of the city?
a ☐ at least one year
b ☐ exactly one year
c ☐ less than one year

2 What does Ayesha say about taxis during her first visit?
a ☐ It was impossible for her to find one.
b ☐ She was not able to use them.
c ☐ They were better than public transportation.

3 Why is Ayesha writing another report about the city?
a ☐ She had been invited to an anniversary party in the city.
b ☐ She has become a professional journalist.
c ☐ She heard that a lot of money had been spent on the city.

4 How has the train station improved since Ayesha's last visit?
a ☐ Men are employed to help her get from the platform to the exit.
b ☐ She can get from the platform to the exit by herself.
c ☐ They have repaired the old elevators on the platform.

5 How many of the ATMs at the station can Ayesha use easily?
a ☐ one b ☐ two c ☐ three

6 How many different forms of transportation did Ayesha use to get around the city?
a ☐ one b ☐ two c ☐ three

c Think about the place where you live. How easy or difficult do you think it might be for wheelchair users to get around your hometown? Make notes about:

- public transportation (Do buses/trains/trams have disabled access?)
- things to do and places to visit. (Is it easy to visit a museum or go shopping?)

Use your notes to write a short review of disabled access for wheelchair users where you live.

CITY MAKES PROGRESS FOR DISABLED

This week is the first anniversary of Mayor Alex Walker's promise to make life in our city easier for disabled people. One year later, we asked disabled athlete Ayesha Omar to tell us about her experiences in the city.

Just over a year ago, *City News* invited me here for the day to do an interview. It turned out to be a visit I will never forget – unfortunately, for all the wrong reasons. As someone in a wheelchair, it was almost impossible for me to get around the city. There was not nearly enough access to public transportation, and I discovered that taxis weren't any better: none of them had the special doors I need to carry my wheelchair. The day was such a nightmare that I decided to write a story about my experience in the paper. After I wrote my story, Mayor Alex Walker promised to make things better in the city and gave $6 million to the project. Last week, I returned to see if the city had improved.

I arrived at the train station early in the morning. One year ago, the station only had stairs up to the exit. That meant that three men had to carry me off the platform, which was by far the most embarrassing thing that happened to me during my last visit. This year, I saw immediately that they had built a new elevator. "Wonderful!" I thought – but then I remembered something: the buttons. On "normal" elevators, the buttons are sometimes too high for a person in a wheelchair. That means I have to ask someone to push the buttons for me. However, the elevator in the station had buttons that were much lower, so I was able to push them myself. I was really pleased.

I decided to take a taxi downtown, so first of all, I needed to get some money from the bank. Again, I am very pleased to say that when I found the line of three ATMs outside the station, one of them was lower than the other two, and so it was the right height for wheelchair users. Later that day, I took a bus and a tram and visited all the main museums, galleries, and shopping centers. There was access for wheelchair users everywhere I went. Things are still not perfect, and there is a long way to go, but I can honestly say that Alex Walker has kept his promise to disabled people in the city!

2 LISTENING

a 06.08 Listen to a conversation between three students – Peeraya, Silvia, and Matt – and check (✓) the correct answers.

1 Which two students are meeting for the first time?
  a ☐ Peeraya and Matt
  b ☐ Peeraya and Silvia
  c ☐ Silvia and Matt
2 How do Peeraya and Silvia know each other?
  a ☐ They are going to Boston together.
  b ☐ They study English together.
  c ☐ They met on vacation in Thailand.
3 Peeraya and Silvia ask Matt to … .
  a ☐ recommend a good, local restaurant
  b ☐ explain how to make clam chowder
  c ☐ tell them the best place to get a burger
4 At the end of the conversation, Peeraya and Silvia … .
  a ☐ agree with Matt's recommendation
  b ☐ ask Matt to recommend something else
  c ☐ decide to ask someone else

b Listen again. Underline the correct words to complete the sentences.

1 Peeraya and Silvia are planning a celebration for *the end of their English class* / *their friend's birthday* / *passing their English exams.*
2 Matt says that he has lived in Boston *for a fairly long time* / *for a really short time* / *all his life.*
3 Peeraya and Silvia think there will be *18* / *20* / *21* people at the celebration.
4 Silvia does not want to go to a *big* / *chain* / *family* restaurant.
5 Both Peeraya and Silvia would like to try *oysters* / *hot and spicy Thai seafood* / *traditional American dishes.*
6 Clam chowder is a traditional *dessert* / *soup* / *vegetarian dish* in Boston.
7 To get to *Bostonia Public House*, Peeraya and Silvia should *turn right* / *turn left* / *go straight on* at the ATM on State Street.

c Write a conversation between two people discussing how to celebrate the end of their English class. Use the questions below to help you.

- How many people will go?
- Where will they go to eat? Will the place be big enough?
- Is anyone in the class a vegetarian?
- Is there any type of food that someone in the class cannot eat (for example, fish)?

Review and extension

1 GRAMMAR

Correct the sentences.

1 You must to arrive 30 minutes before the exam starts.
  You must arrive 30 minutes before the exam starts.
2 I think this is the better Greek restaurant in New York.
3 Last night we must take a taxi because we missed the bus.
4 His house is more close to the university than yours.
5 You must not parking outside that school.
6 He's more taller than his older brother.
7 You don't have to feed the animals in the zoo – it's forbidden.
8 I think Spanish is easyer to learn than English.

2 VOCABULARY

Correct the sentences and questions.

1 On the first day of vacation, his new walk shoes hurt his feet.
  On the first day of vacation, his new walking shoes hurt his feet.
2 Can I borrow your spoon so I can mix my coffee?
3 She said we should read the tour guide to avoid a lot of culture shock.
4 You need to fry the onion and garlic before you put it in the pan.
5 Mash the lemon and pour the juice over the fish.
6 If you put in too much sugar, it will be too sour to drink.

3 WORDPOWER *go*

Match 1–6 with a–f to make sentences.

1 [d] I don't think anything can go
2 ☐ My English exam went
3 ☐ Unfortunately, all the tickets were gone
4 ☐ The stairs next to the elevator go
5 ☐ The tie you bought yesterday goes
6 ☐ My father's hair has all gone

a really well with your blue shirt.
b down to the parking lot.
c by the time we got there.
d wrong because it's a great plan.
e gray now, but it was blond when he was young.
f really well. I think I passed.

REVIEW YOUR PROGRESS

Look again at Review Your Progress on p. 78 of the Student's Book. How well can you do these things now?
3 = very well 2 = well 1 = not so well

I CAN …	
talk about advice and rules	☐
describe food	☐
ask for and give recommendations	☐
write a review of a restaurant or café.	☐

7A IT MIGHT BE A VACATION HOME

1 GRAMMAR Modals of deduction

a Match 1–7 with a–g to make pairs of sentences.

1 [g] They may have some relatives in Miami.
2 [ ] She can't live in that tiny apartment.
3 [ ] Their car's outside the house, but I haven't seen them for a few days.
4 [ ] There are a lot of people in our neighbor's yard.
5 [ ] Why is Sam wearing a suit and tie?
6 [ ] She can't still be living with her parents.
7 [ ] He might not have a well-paying job right now.

a They could be away on vacation.
b That's why he's not taking his family on vacation this year.
c They might be having a party.
d She's nearly 40 years old.
e She told me it had four bedrooms and two bathrooms.
f He must be going to his job interview.
g Maybe that's why they go there every January.

b Underline the correct words to complete the conversation.

A Some new people have just moved into the house next door.
B Yes, I know. I saw them yesterday when they arrived. I think they're French.
A No, they [1]*mustn't / can't / must* be French. I heard them speaking a language that sounded like Spanish.
B Oh, really? They [2]*can't / couldn't / might* help me with my French homework, then.
A They [3]*must not / could / can't* be Portuguese.
B That's true – Portuguese and Spanish sound alike.
A Is it a family or a couple?
B It [4]*must / can't / couldn't* be a family. They [5]*couldn't / must / must not* have two or three children.
A How do you know that?
B Because I saw some children's bikes in their yard. Also, there was another woman in the car when they arrived yesterday – she was older than the mother.
A She [6]*might / can / couldn't* be the children's grandmother.
B No, she [7]*can / must not / can't* be their grandmother. She looked too young.
A Or she [8]*must / can't / could* be their aunt? Or she [9]*can't / might not / can* be a relative at all. She [10]*may / can't / can* be just a friend. She [11]*can't / might / can* be helping them to unpack their things.
B Why don't we go and say hello?
A But they [12]*might not / can't / couldn't* speak English – it [13]*can't / could / must not* be really embarrassing.
B They [14]*can't / couldn't / must* speak English. I just saw them speaking to one of the neighbors, and they seemed to understand each other.

c 07.01 Listen and check.

2 VOCABULARY Buildings

a Complete the crossword puzzle.

→ Across
3 I'd like to live in a friendly and safe ________ that has a good school for my children.
5 When you get to my apartment building, ring the ________ and I'll let you in.
7 Something is wrong with the ________ on the door or with my key. I can't get in my apartment!
8 We had a beautiful hotel room with a large ________ where I could read my book and get a tan.

↓ Down
1 I had a great ___view___ of the ocean from my hotel window.
2 His house is in a very convenient ________. He can walk downtown in five minutes.
4 A lot of American houses have a large ________ below the house where the children can watch TV and play.
6 My office is on the 22nd ________, so I take the elevator.

b Underline the correct words to complete the sentences.

1 At the top of my house, there's *a balcony / an attic / a basement* where we keep all the things we don't use anymore.
2 When I lived in Rome, I *located / hired / rented* a tiny *balcony / apartment / landing* that only had two rooms.
3 Go up the stairs to the *landing / hall / basement* on the second *balcony / step / floor*. My bedroom is the first on the right.
4 The *principal / front / in front of* door has two *locks / views / steps*, so take both keys when you leave the house.
5 I'm moving *off / out of / away* this apartment next Saturday and moving *in / on / into* my new apartment on Sunday.
6 I love to sit outside on the *balcony / landing / first floor*. It has a great *lock / view / window*.

3 PRONUNCIATION Modal verbs: final /t/ sounds

a 07.02 Listen. Check (✓) the sentences where you clearly hear the final /t/ of the modal verbs.

1 [✓] He mus**t** have rich parents.
2 [ ] She can'**t** be studying for her exams tonight.
3 [ ] They migh**t** enjoy going to the zoo.
4 [ ] We mus**t** be pretty close to downtown now.
5 [ ] John mus**t** earn a lot more money than she does.

7B THERE ARE PLENTY OF THINGS TO DO

1 GRAMMAR Quantifiers

a Complete the sentences with the words in the box.

too many	plenty	~~many~~	no
some	a few	little	enough (x2)

1 She doesn't have __many__ clothes for work, so she needs to buy ______.
2 There isn't ______ time to eat before the movie.
3 There are ______ cars on the roads these days.
4 We have ______ of time before the movie starts, so let's go get coffee.
5 He knows quite ______ people in Quito, so he won't be lonely.
6 I'm sorry, but there are ______ tickets left for tonight's show.
7 She isn't fluent ______ to become a Spanish teacher yet.
8 I have very ______ money left, so I'm not going out tonight.

b Correct the sentences.

1 I'm late because there was much traffic downtown.
<u>*I'm late because there was a lot of traffic downtown.*</u>
2 Unfortunately, there aren't no good restaurants near here.
______
3 He won't pass his exams because he hasn't worked enough hard this year.
______
4 **A** Is there many milk left?
______
B Yes, we've got plenty of.
______
5 There were too much people at the bus stop to get on the bus.
______
6 There are too little eggs in the fridge to make an omelet.
______
7 My father's too much old to play tennis these days.
______
8 She made lot of mistakes in her translation.
______

2 VOCABULARY Verbs and prepositions

a <u>Underline</u> the correct words to complete the sentences.

1 He paid *about* / *around* / <u>*for*</u> the clothes with his credit card.
2 I complained to the receptionist *about* / *for* / *from* the dirty towels in my room.
3 They apologized to their teacher *about* / *for* / *with* not doing all their homework.
4 We try to recycle all of our trash because we care *for* / *about* / *with* the environment.
5 If you get into trouble, you can always depend *about* / *for* / *on* your family to help you.
6 She's thinking *about* / *in* / *at* her boyfriend.
7 It was very hard for the children to cope *about* / *with* / *for* their parents' divorce.
8 After five years in Tokyo, he succeeded *for* / *on* / *in* learning Japanese.

b Complete the sentences with one word from each of the boxes.

rely	complained	~~believe~~	apologized
belongs	argued	cope	worried

to (x2)	with (x2)	about (x2)	~~in~~	on

1 When I was little, I used to __believe__ __in__ ghosts.
2 She's finding it hard to ______ ______ the stress of her new job.
3 I ______ ______ Jane for forgetting her birthday.
4 You can always ______ ______ the subway because the trains run very regularly.
5 Dan's getting ______ ______ his job because his company wants to save money.
6 I think that cat ______ ______ one of my neighbors.
7 He went across the street and ______ ______ the noise his neighbor was making.
8 After they saw how expensive their dinner was, they ______ ______ the server about the check.

7C EVERYDAY ENGLISH

Is there anything we can do to help?

1 USEFUL LANGUAGE Offers, requests, and permission

a Match questions 1–6 with responses a–f.

1 [d] Do you think you could help me with the shopping bags?
2 [ ] Is there anything I can do to help?
3 [ ] Do you think I could take a quick shower?
4 [ ] May I use your phone?
5 [ ] Do you mind if I watch the news on TV?
6 [ ] Would you mind taking your shoes off?

a Not at all. Let me turn it on for you.
b No, not at all. Where should I leave them?
c Yes, of course. Here you go.
d Sure, I'll take them to the car for you.
e Yes, of course. Let me get you a towel.
f Yes, there is, actually. Could you set the table for me?

b 07.03 Listen and check.

c Complete the responses with the words in the box. There is one extra word you do not need.

~~course~~ great mind sure let control thank you

1 **A** Do you think I could borrow your camera tomorrow?
B Yes, of _course_. It's in the living room. Here you go.
2 **A** I'm sorry about the problem with your computer. Is there anything I can do to help?
B It's all under ________. I think I can fix it.
3 **A** Do you think you could give me a hand with this math homework?
B ________. Let me have a look at it.
4 **A** Are you OK in the kitchen? Let me help you.
B Oh, ________.
5 **A** Is there anything I can do for the party? I could organize some games for the kids.
B That would be ________, thanks.
6 **A** I'm hungry. Is it OK if I have a sandwich?
B ________ me make you something special for lunch.

d Underline the correct words to complete the sentences.

1 Would you mind *open* / *opening* / *to open* that door for me?
2 Would you *excuse* / *excused* / *excusing* me for a moment?
3 **A** Do you think *I'd* / *I would* / *I could* have some coffee?
B Yes, of course. *I should* / *I'll* / *I would* make some for you.
4 **A** Would you mind if *I used* / *I use* / *I'll use* your bathroom?
B Not at all. *Leave* / *Let* / *Allow* me show you where it is.
5 Is there *anything* / *nothing* / *a thing* I can do to help?
6 Excuse me. Do you think you *will* / *could* / *would* turn the music down a little, please? It's really hard to talk in here.

e 07.04 Listen and check.

2 PRONUNCIATION Sounding polite

a 07.05 Listen to the pairs of questions. Check (✓) the question that sounds more polite: a or b.

1 a Would you mind getting me some more water? [✓]
b Would you mind getting me some more water? [ ]
2 a Do you think you could lend me some money? [ ]
b Do you think you could lend me some money? [ ]
3 a Can I make myself some coffee? [ ]
b Can I make myself some coffee? [ ]
4 a Do you think I could borrow your car? [ ]
b Do you think I could borrow your car? [ ]
5 a Do you mind if I make a quick phone call? [ ]
b Do you mind if I make a quick phone call? [ ]

7D SKILLS FOR WRITING
Make yourselves at home

1 READING

a Read the note and check (✓) the correct answer.

a ☐ Sarah hasn't left any food in her fridge for Paul.
b ☐ You can't walk downtown from Sarah's house.
c ☐ Paul's children won't get bored in Grand Forks.
d ☐ You can go swimming at Lincoln Drive Park.

b Read the note again. Are the sentences true or false?

1 Paul needs to go to the supermarket to buy some bread for breakfast.
2 There aren't any big supermarkets in Grand Forks.
3 It's easy to take the bus from Sarah's house to downtown.
4 Paul's children would enjoy a visit to the Children's Museum.
5 Paul can't go swimming with his children in Grand Forks.

Hi Paul!

Welcome to Grand Forks! Hope you had a good trip from Minneapolis and that it wasn't difficult to find my house and get the keys from my next-door neighbor.

Help yourself to anything you find in the fridge and the kitchen cupboards. For breakfast tomorrow morning, you can have cereal with milk. Otherwise, there's plenty of bread to make toast, and you'll find butter and strawberry jam in the fridge.

If you need to go shopping for lunch or dinner, the nearest supermarket is on Washington Street and 8th Avenue, a big street that goes downtown. You probably passed it on your way to my house. Alternatively, you can drive to Hugo's Family Marketplace on Columbia Road, which has everything you need.

By the way, you can get downtown by taking the bus from the end of my street. The bus runs every fifteen minutes or so. Another option is to walk. It takes about 25 minutes to walk downtown from here, but it's good exercise.

There are plenty of things to do and see in Grand Forks. You can take the kids to Greenway along Red River, where you can have a picnic and explore the different parks. Another possibility is to visit the Children's Museum. I think they'll enjoy going to both places. Apart from that, there are a lot of good stores downtown and also plenty of nice coffee shops and restaurants if you prefer to eat out.

Finally, if you need some exercise, there's a big swimming pool on Central Avenue. Alternatively, if the weather's nice, you and the kids can go bike riding in Lincoln Drive Park. I have extra bikes in the garage.

Anyway, enjoy your stay! Talk to you soon.

Love,

Sarah

2 WRITING SKILLS Offering choices

a Use one of the words or phrases in the box to connect the sentences. Make any necessary changes. There is more than one possible answer.

Another option is	Otherwise	Alternatively
Apart from that	Another possibility is	

1 You can take the train from here to Granada. Or there is a bus that runs every two hours.
<u>You can take the train from here to Granada. Apart from that, there is a bus that runs every two hours.</u>

2 There's a good store at the end of my street. You could also go to the huge supermarket, which is just before you get to the highway.
____

3 You can get a good view of London from the London Eye. Or you can go to the top of The Shard building.
____

4 I suggest you go to the beach early in the morning, before it gets too hot. You could also go late in the afternoon.
____

5 Why don't you go to that Italian restaurant next to Washington High School? Or you could try that new Japanese restaurant near the new supermarket.
____

3 WRITING

a Read the notes. Write a note to Pascale, the babysitter who is going to look after your two young children this evening.

Note to Pascale

1) Drinks & snacks
- Tea & coffee by fridge. Hot chocolate in cupboard.
- Chocolate cookies on table. Cheesecake in fridge.

2) Dinner for children
- Tomato soup & chicken nuggets in fridge. Sandwiches.

3) Entertainment
- OK to watch TV (both like Spongebob Squarepants)
- Favorite movies are Toy Story 4 & Finding Nemo.

4) Bedtime
- Read bedtime story e.g., Harry Potter / The Lion, the Witch and the Wardrobe.

5) If any problems, call:
- (614) 555-3192 (Me)
- (614) 555-3871 (Other person's cell phone.)

UNIT 7
Reading and listening extension

1 READING

a Read the article. Match paragraphs A–D with functions 1–6. There are two extra functions you do not need.

☐ Paragraph A ☐ Paragraph C
☐ Paragraph B ☐ Paragraph D

1 to describe how Detroit changed
2 to explain that education in Detroit has become worse
3 to make a prediction about the future of Detroit
4 to show that Detroit helped a singer become famous
5 to show that Detroit might be improving
6 to show the reader why Detroit is an important place

b Read the article again and put the information in the order that it's presented.

☐ a possible benefit of recent changes to Detroit
☐ businessmen whose relatives are from Detroit
☐ how old parts of Detroit have changed recently
☐ other names for Detroit
☐ popular songs that came from Detroit
1 a businessman who made Detroit famous
☐ the number of people who live in Detroit
☐ the number of people who used to live in Detroit
☐ the way people might think about Detroit in the future
☐ where many people in the city used to work

c Think about your hometown or another place that you know well. Write notes about:

- where it is
- how old it is
- some famous people who have lived there
- some things it is famous for / things that you can only find in that place
- some important changes that have happened there in the last 50 years.

Write a short essay about this place.

DETROIT: A TALE OF TWO CITIES

A **DETROIT** was at one time one of the most famous cities in the United States, and perhaps even the world. This was the city where Henry Ford built the Ford Motor Company in 1903, and it didn't take long for Detroit to become known as "Motor City." Later, "Motor City" became simply "Motown," which was, of course, the name given to the popular American music of the 1960s and '70s that came out of the city, including Diana Ross and the Supremes, who had hits like "Where Did Our Love Go?", and Stevie Wonder, whose songs included "Superstition." Today, however, Detroit is a very different place.

B In 1950, the city had a population of 1.8 million, and there were nearly 300,000 men and women working in its car factories. Nowadays, that population is just 700,000, and only a small number of people have jobs connected with the car industry. So many people moved out of Detroit after 2001 that by 2010, more than a third of Detroit's houses, factories, and schools were empty. In a lot of neighborhoods, not only was there no more noise from the traffic, but there was also no more music. The city was so cold and dark that many people thought the city had died. Then businessmen John Hantz and Michael Score moved in.

C Hantz and Score, who both have family connections in Detroit, cared about what was happening there. They also both believed in the same very simple idea – urban farms. Together, they bought a lot of empty land in the city and then pulled down 50 old houses. Instead of broken buildings, there are now fields of trees. Once Hantz and Score had succeeded in showing what could be done with all that empty land, a lot of other people started to create their own gardens. Men and women who used to build cars and trucks are now planting fruit and vegetables. And now something even better has happened.

D In the first ten years of the 21st century, crime increased and many residents became worried about safety on the streets at night. But now, incredibly, crime has fallen and many residents believe this must be due to the new urban farms and gardens. Although it has not been proven whether the new green spaces are the reason that crime has gone down, you can be sure that no one in the city is complaining about it! Perhaps this could be a change other cities around the world could learn from, and it might not be long before "Motor City" becomes known as "Green City."

2 LISTENING

a 07.06 Listen to a group of friends talking. Match 1–6 with a–f to make sentences.

1 [b] They must
2 [ ] They can't
3 [ ] One of them has to
4 [ ] Some of them have to
5 [ ] Katia is the person who is
6 [ ] Ben is the person who is

a describe a place to the others.
b be playing some kind of game.
c talking about a house.
d explaining how to play the game.
e draw something.
f be in the college library.

b Listen to the conversation again. Check (✓) the correct answer.

1 On her turn, Katia gets … .
a [ ] three b [ ] twelve c [ ] sixteen

2 Luis and Daniela have to draw what she describes … .
a [ ] on the same piece of paper
b [ ] using a special kind of pencil
c [ ] without looking at their picture

3 Where would Katia's dream home be?
a [ ] by the ocean
b [ ] in a small town
c [ ] in a big city

4 What would Katia be able to see from her dream home?
a [ ] a beautiful mountain lake
b [ ] her favorite shopping mall
c [ ] some famous places

5 What would Katia's dream home be?
a [ ] an apartment
b [ ] a cottage
c [ ] a palace

6 What size would Katia's dream home be?
a [ ] small and cozy
b [ ] medium-sized
c [ ] very large

7 Where would Katia like to have picnics and parties?
a [ ] on the Seine River
b [ ] on her balcony
c [ ] in her kitchen

8 What kind of kitchen would she like to have?
a [ ] a kitchen with gold tables and chairs
b [ ] a modern kitchen with lots of technology
c [ ] an old-fashioned kitchen

c Write about your dream home. Remember to include:

- the location
- the views
- the size / number of rooms
- the type of home
- what the building looks like.

Review and extension

1 GRAMMAR

Correct the sentences.

1 He's not answering the phone, so he must to be away on vacation.
He's not answering the phone, so he must be away on vacation.
2 George isn't enough good at soccer to play for the school team.
3 She won't be the manager – she looks too young!
4 There's much traffic downtown during rush hour.
5 They must not be doing their homework right now – it's almost midnight!
6 The math exam was too much difficult for most of the people in my class.

2 VOCABULARY

Correct the sentences.

1 His new apartment is in an excellent place. There's a beautiful park on his street, and the metro station's only a five-minute walk away.
His new apartment is in an excellent location. There's a beautiful park on his street, and the metro station's only a five-minute walk away.
2 She complainted to the server about the dirty glass.
3 I can't afford to buy an apartment right now, so I'm going to hire an apartment downtown.
4 Don't worry about the check. I'll pay the meal.
5 I live in a really nice neighbor – everyone's very friendly.
6 When he told me about the accident, I didn't believe in him at first.

3 WORDPOWER *over*

Match 1–6 with a–f to make sentences.

1 [b] I've only seen her three or four times over
2 [ ] After about three minutes, turn the steak over
3 [ ] It usually takes about seven hours to fly over
4 [ ] If the game starts at 3 o'clock, it should be over
5 [ ] By 2050, there will be over
6 [ ] There's glass all over

a the Atlantic from New York to London.
b the past 20 years.
c and cook the other side.
d the floor because I dropped a vase.
e 10 billion people living on the planet.
f by a quarter to five.

REVIEW YOUR PROGRESS

Look again at Review Your Progress on p. 90 of the Student's Book. How well can you do these things now?
3 = very well 2 = well 1 = not so well

I CAN …	
describe a building	[ ]
describe a town or city	[ ]
make offers and requests and ask for permission	[ ]
write a note with useful information.	[ ]

8A I REPLIED THAT I'D BEEN BORED WITH MY MUSIC

1 GRAMMAR Reported speech (statements and questions)

a Correct the mistakes in the sentences with reported speech. There may be more than one mistake in each sentence.

1 Yesterday, John said, "I'm going to call my mother this evening."
Yesterday, John said me that he's going to call my mother this evening.
Yesterday, John told me that he was going to call his mother that evening.

2 "You should wait behind this line until it is your turn."
She said I should wait behind this line until it is your turn.
____

3 "Are you going to the meeting this afternoon?"
When I talked to her last Friday, she asked to me if I'm going to the meeting this afternoon.
____

4 "He might be about 50 years old."
She said me he might be about 50 years old.
____

5 He said, "I'm sorry, but I can't find your post on Facebook."
He told he's sorry, but he can't find my post on Facebook.
____

6 "Did you see your uncle when you were in New York last month?"
She asked me did I see your uncle when I were in New York last month.
____

7 "Goodbye, Anna. I'll see you next week."
He told Anna he will see me next week.
____

b Complete the reported speech with the correct verb form. Change the tense where possible.

1 "Mandy's coming to stay with me next week."
She said that Mandy was coming to stay with her the next week.

2 "Martin has just sent me a text."
He said that ______________________.

3 "I'll call you when I get home from work."
He told me ______________________.

4 "Are you going to send your brother an email this afternoon?"
He asked me ______________________.

5 "Why can't you lend me some money?"
She asked me ______________________.

6 "You need to stop writing immediately and give me your papers."
The teacher said that we
______________________.

7 "I want you to take these flowers to your grandmother."
She told me ______________________.

2 VOCABULARY Sharing information

a Underline the correct words to complete the sentences.

1 She *posted / sent / delivered* photos on Instagram of her trip to Istanbul.
2 I think it's a good idea for us to *hold / deliver / brainstorm* ideas before the meeting with our boss.
3 Did you see all the flyers about the Black Friday sale the electronics store *sent / gain / got* last week?
4 He told me he *put up / sent / posted* her two texts this morning, but she still hasn't replied.
5 Why don't you *have / talk / brainstorm* a chat with your coworker before you complain to your boss about him?
6 We saw someone *putting up / posting / sending* a poster at school about a movie night on Friday.
7 Have you *listened to / created / made* that podcast I told you about yet? This week's episode was really funny.
8 The human resources department should *give / hold / subscribe to* a meeting about these new changes at the office.

b Complete the crossword puzzle.

→ Across

1 This podcast releases a new ____________ every Monday. It's my favorite part of starting the week!
5 I don't like this news site. The items are updated only once a day, so I never know if I've missed an important story.
7 I prefer to have a phone ____________ instead of writing an email for important work communication. It's nice to hear your client's voice sometimes.
8 I found a new ____________ of news podcasts. They're informative and entertaining at the same time!

↓ Down

2 Look at this ____________ I'm going to put up at work. We're going to have a huge sale!
3 Someone from the new Mexican restaurant across the street ____________ this flyer with their menu. It looks good!
4 If I ____________ to this podcast, then the new episodes will download to my phone automatically.
6 I check the ____________ on my Facebook account all the time. That way I always know what my friends are doing!

8B SETTING UP THE WEBSITE WAS EASY

1 GRAMMAR Verb patterns

a Complete the sentences with the *-ing* form or the *to* + infinitive form of the verb in parentheses.

1 __Reading__ (read) a good book is an excellent way to relax before ________ (go) to bed.
2 She remembered ________ (see) the movie in the movie theater when she was a little girl.
3 It will be extremely difficult ________ (get) a ticket for the World Cup Final.
4 We promised ________ (come) back at the same time the next day.
5 He didn't enjoy ________ (visit) his grandparents.
6 Would you mind ________ (wait) here for me while I get changed?
7 Instead of ________ (go) to the bookstore, they went to the library ________ (see) if they could borrow a copy of *The Great Gatsby*.
8 In my opinion, it's not worth ________ (pay) to see the new Spielberg movie.

b Correct the sentences.

1 I called Philip ask him if he wanted playing tennis this weekend.
__I called Philip to ask him if he wanted to play tennis this weekend.__
2 Don't forget giving me back my book when you finish read it.
____
3 He admitted to steal the woman's bag.
____
4 We hoped finding a good place to eat on one of the streets near the train station.
____
5 He threatened telling my parents what I had done.
____
6 It's really important teach your children how crossing the street safely.
____
7 She didn't know which book buying her brother for his birthday.
____
8 You promised helping me with my homework!
____

2 VOCABULARY Reporting verbs

a Complete the sentences with the correct form of the verbs in the box.

warn ~~advise~~ refuse offer
agree suggest

1 "You should apply for the marketing director position."
He __advised__ her to apply for the marketing director position.
2 "Yes, that's fine. I'm happy to sell you my car for $5,000."
She ________ to sell me her car for $5,000.
3 "Why don't we go to the beach tomorrow?"
He ________ going to the beach the next day.
4 "Be careful! Don't touch that plate – it's hot!"
He ________ her not to touch the plate because it was hot.
5 "I'm not going to lend you any more money."
I ________ to lend her any more money.
6 "If you like, I can give you a lift to the bus station."
He ________ to give us a lift to the bus station.

b Underline the correct words to complete the sentences.

1 She doesn't know where the bathroom is, so she's going to *advise* / *ask* / *threaten* the server.
2 Jack's parents don't usually allow him to come home after midnight, but he *promised* / *recommended* / *warned* he would text them at 1 a.m. to let them know he was OK.
3 What beaches do you *recommend* / *persuade* / *ask* visiting while we are in Florida?
4 Their neighbor *persuaded* / *advised* / *threatened* to call the police if they didn't turn down the music.
5 The radio *advised* / *warned* / *promised* us of the snow and traffic on the highway.
6 Casey didn't want to go to the concert, but his girlfriend *offered* / *persuaded* / *threatened* him to go. He had a great time.

c 08.01 Listen and check.

8C EVERYDAY ENGLISH

On the whole, I prefer writing about current events

1 USEFUL LANGUAGE Generalizing

a Put the words in the right order to make sentences.

1 be / movie / of / honest, / the / was / boring / kind / to .
To be honest, the movie was kind of boring.
2 my / tend / Americans / be / experience, / friendly / to / very / in .
____
3 generally / that / thing / of / I / like / kind / don't .
____
4 whole, / I / his / liked / movie / the / new / on .
____
5 songs / of / his / can / depressing / some / kind of / be .
____
6 a / coffee / Italian / is / rule, / excellent / as .
____

b 08.02 Listen and check.

2 CONVERSATION SKILLS Being vague

a Complete the sentences with the words in the box.

whole stuff ~~that~~ couple sort

1 He likes hip hop and rap music – you know, stuff like *that*.
2 We had a __________ of days when it was cloudy and rainy, but on the __________, we had pretty good weather.
3 Don't touch all that __________ in his office, please.
4 She likes watching documentaries about animals and nature and that __________ of thing.

b 08.03 Listen and check.

3 PRONUNCIATION Sound and spelling: /h/ and /w/

a 08.04 Listen to the sentences. Put the words in **bold** in the correct columns.

1 **When** did you last see her?
2 They **went** the **wrong way** and got lost.
3 **Whose** suitcase was the **heaviest**?
4 I **wrote** a long email to my uncle in Scotland.
5 I didn't know **which** book to get my **husband**.
6 She **had** to wait two **hours** for the next train to Portland.

/h/ (e.g., *hot*)	/w/ (e.g., *with*)	First letter silent (e.g., *honest*)

b 08.05 Listen and check.

8D SKILLS FOR WRITING

Fortunately, everything was all right

1 READING

a Read the email and check (✓) the correct answer.

a ☐ The alligator attacked Pongo and broke his leg.
b ☐ The alligator bit Pam and broke her leg.
c ☐ Pongo was afraid of the alligator and didn't stay with Pam.
d ☐ Pam broke her leg while she was walking with Pongo.

I read an amazing story in the newspaper this morning about a dog named Pongo who saved his owner's life in Florida. It seems that his owner, Pam Evans, who is 79 years old, was walking near a lake when she fell down and broke her leg. Unfortunately, she couldn't move and didn't have a cell phone, so she couldn't call for help. At that moment, a huge alligator came out of the lake and started walking toward Pam, threatening to attack her. Incredibly, Pongo wasn't frightened by the alligator and, apparently, he started fighting it to try and protect Pam. Amazingly, after a few minutes, the alligator gave up trying to attack Pam and went back into the lake. Fortunately, a man who was near the lake with his dog heard Pongo barking and came to rescue Pam. It seems that he then called for an ambulance, which immediately took Pam to the hospital. Luckily, neither Pam nor Pongo was hurt in the attack, and Pam has now made a full recovery.

b Read the email again. Are the sentences true or false?

1 Pam Evans has a dog named Pongo.
2 Pam couldn't call for help because her cell phone was broken.
3 When Pongo saw the alligator, he was very frightened and ran away.
4 The man near the lake called for an ambulance.
5 Pongo was seriously injured by the alligator.

2 WRITING SKILLS

Summarizing information

a Use one of the words in the box to connect the sentences. Make any necessary changes. Sometimes there is more than one possible answer.

before	who	but	with	and	that

1 The man spent several hours looking for his son. Unfortunately, he couldn't find him anywhere.
The man spent several hours looking for his son, but unfortunately, he couldn't find him anywhere.

2 I heard a story on the radio about an elephant. Apparently, it sat on a car in a safari park.

______

3 The 12-year-old girl took her father's motorcycle. She rode it for 40 km on the highway. The police stopped her near Milwaukee.

______

4 The woman hit the teenager hard on his head with her umbrella. Then she used his cell phone to call the police.

______

5 Amanda escaped from the burning building by breaking a window. She used her shoe to break the window.

______

6 There was an incredible story on the news about a baby in China. She fell from a fourth-floor window. She wasn't hurt because a man in the street caught her.

______

3 WRITING

a Read the notes. Write the story.

FAMILY'S LUCKY ESCAPE WHEN CAR CRASHES INTO HOUSE

Car crashed into house. Manchester.
Family watching TV in living room at time of accident. Heard loud noise.
Driver lost control of car. Drove straight through front door. Stopped 2 meters from kitchen.
No one seriously hurt. Driver & 3 passengers only minor injuries.
Police were called. Arrived 5 minutes later.
Front of house badly damaged.
Car removed. Took firefighters 6 hours.

UNIT 8
Reading and listening extension

1 READING

a Read the article and check (✓) the correct answers.

1 Why has the article been written?
  a ☐ to encourage more students to take courses in journalism
  b ☐ to explain why careers in journalism have become popular
  c ☐ to show the advantages and disadvantages of a career in journalism

2 Who has the article been written for?
  a ☐ owners of news organizations
  b ☐ professional journalists
  c ☐ students who study journalism

3 Which of these things do Mercedes and Shanna have in common?
  a ☐ They both earn good money at their job.
  b ☐ They both love their work.
  c ☐ They both studied journalism in college.

4 Mercedes and Shanna both agree that people who want to become journalists … .
  a ☐ need to travel all over the world
  b ☐ should be really interested in journalism
  c ☐ will have to work on weekends

b Read the text again and check (✓) the correct answers.

Who … ?	Mercedes	Shanna	Neither Mercedes nor Shanna
1 works when they are traveling	✓		
2 enjoys thinking about the readers of their stories			
3 has a parent who was also a journalist			
4 does not sleep very much			
5 won a prize for journalism while in college			
6 often writes more than one story in a day			
7 always knew they wanted to be a journalist			
8 became a journalist by accident			
9 takes their own photos for their stories			
10 has no free time in the mornings			
11 works from home			
12 writes stories of 1,000 words			

c Read the notice from a student magazine. Write a short article.

We are looking for people to tell us about their work or study experiences. We would like you to write a short article explaining:

- what your job is or what you are studying
- why you have chosen the job or major
- a typical day at work or at college.

CAREERS for LIFE

A report this week announced that journalism courses are now more popular than ever with students. But what is it like to work as a journalist?

Here, two young journalists tell* Careers for Life *about their experience.

THE NEWSPAPER JOURNALIST

Mercedes Alvarado, 28

A typical day for me starts at 7 a.m. The morning is always the hardest part of the day because I have to work all the time without any breaks. I only have about seven or eight hours to finish a story, and there is a lot to do in that time.

First, I have to interview people for the story, and sometimes that means traveling a long way. I usually go by train so that I can keep on working on my laptop. I also need to think about photos for the story. These days, I usually buy pictures from a photo agency, but sometimes a photographer goes with me on a story. I usually have to write a story of about 1,000 words, and it can be very difficult to do that in only a few hours. By 4 p.m., I'm usually exhausted, but I don't normally leave work until 5 p.m.

I have wanted to be a journalist since I was five years old, and I studied journalism in college, so working for a newspaper has been a dream come true. Journalism is a great career but can be a very stressful one that does not pay very well. Anyone who is thinking of becoming a journalist needs to know that.

THE BUSINESS BLOGGER

Shanna Kaufman, 26

I had never had any plans to become a journalist, but then I started my business blog when I was still in college. I wasn't enjoying life as a student, so when a news organization offered to pay me for my reports, I immediately accepted. I eventually quit college to blog full time, even though I've never actually had any training as a reporter.

My day starts at 4 a.m. when I check Twitter in bed to find out what has happened around the world during the night. I start preparing my first report at around 4:30 a.m., and it is usually finished and on my website by 5:30 a.m. On a normal day, I can expect to write maybe five or six reports, and I usually manage to sell at least two or three of them to news agencies. It's really exciting when an agency from another country buys one of my reports. I love the idea that something that I wrote in my kitchen is being read by someone in Dubai or London.

I make good money, but I work hard for it. I often don't go to bed until 11 p.m., and I usually work seven days a week. I would say that unless you are really in love with journalism, this is not a career for you.

2 LISTENING

a 08.06 Listen to a conversation between two friends, Karina and Eva. Are the sentences true or false?

1 One of the women bought a painting.
2 One of the women bought something that she is not happy with.
3 One of the women has been in an argument at a store.
4 One of the women has bought a pair of boots.
5 One of the women has some good news.
6 One of the women is an artist.
7 One of the women is complaining about something.
8 One of the women is the manager of a store.

b Listen to the conversation again and check (✓) the correct answers.

1 When did Karina buy the boots?
 a ☐ in the morning
 b ☐ yesterday
 c ☐ last week
2 Why did Karina think the boots were a good value?
 a ☐ They were half price.
 b ☐ They were designer boots.
 c ☐ They only cost $50.
3 The problem was that Karina was given boots… .
 a ☐ that had been damaged
 b ☐ of the wrong size
 c ☐ in white instead of brown
4 Karina didn't notice the problem until later because the sales assistant … .
 a ☐ didn't open the box for her
 b ☐ hid the problem from her
 c ☐ gave her the wrong box
5 The manager of the store … .
 a ☐ offered to give Karina another pair of boots
 b ☐ promised to give Karina a refund
 c ☐ refused to give Karina her money back
6 What is Karina going to do next?
 a ☐ She is going to call the police.
 b ☐ She is not sure what to do next.
 c ☐ She is going to sell the boots.

c Write a conversation between two people who are Karina's friends. Person A tells Person B what happened to Karina; Person B asks questions. Listen to the conversation again, and write notes to help you retell the story.

Review and extension

1 GRAMMAR

Correct the sentences.

1 She said me she didn't like horror movies.
 She told me she didn't like horror movies.
2 They asked me was I going to the soccer game.
3 He has agreed taking us to the airport.
4 When I called him last night, he said he has just finished his exams.
5 She advised me not tell anyone about our meeting.
6 Yesterday, he told he would help me with my homework.
7 I'm really looking forward to see you on Sunday.

2 VOCABULARY

Correct the sentences.

1 You should subscribe this new podcast series.
 You should subscribe to this new podcast series.
2 I suggest posting a text before you call her.
3 Do you have time to hold a chat later today?
4 He adviced me to buy a new laptop because mine is over five years old.
5 I subscribed that podcast because I liked the name.
6 She asked us that she would send an email when she arrived.
7 We ought to branstorm some ideas this morning.

3 WORDPOWER *in / on + noun*

Underline the correct words to complete the sentences.

1 There are some beautiful photos of Venice *in* / *on* this magazine.
2 I sent him a message *in* / *on* Facebook, but he hasn't replied yet.
3 It's better to watch this movie *in* / *on* a big screen at the movie theater.
4 You always look so pretty *in* / *on* photos!
5 There's always an easy crossword *in* / *on* my newspaper.
6 Is there anything good *in* / *on* TV tonight?
7 Can you pay me *in* / *on* cash, please?
8 Do you have this T-shirt *in* / *on* a larger size?

REVIEW YOUR PROGRESS

Look again at Review Your Progress on p. 102 of the Student's Book. How well can you do these things now?
3 = very well 2 = well 1 = not so well

I CAN …	
talk about podcasts	☐
talk about what other people say	☐
generalize and be vague	☐
write an email summary of a news story.	☐

9A BINGE WATCHING HAS BEEN CRITICIZED BY DOCTORS

1 GRAMMAR The passive

a Put the words in the correct order to make passive sentences.

1 3D cameras / new / will / *Star Wars* / the / filmed / movie / be / with .
The new Star Wars movie will be filmed with 3D cameras.
2 by / directed / Steven Spielberg / was / the movie / *Ready Player One* .
______
3 the / been / come / have / told / to / at / back / 3 p.m. / actors .
______
4 every / are / movies / made / Bollywood / year / in / 1,000 .
______
5 seen / 35 million / was / in / people / its first two weeks / by / the movie *Avatar* .
______
6 interviewed / on / right now / the / being / TV / president / is .
______
7 cars / every / 200,000 / produced / new factory / year / by / are / our .
______
8 used / this old / is / house / in / being / movie / the .
______

b Rewrite the sentences. Use the passive.

1 In the 1990s, they built 250,000 new houses every year.
In the 1990s, 250,000 new houses were built every year.
2 They grow five different varieties of orange in this region.
Five ______
3 The government will give students a loan to pay for their college tuition.
Students ______
4 They are creating the special effects with the latest animation software.
The special effects ______
5 They've asked the actors to give some of their money to charity.
The actors ______
6 He was driving the car really fast when the accident happened.
The car ______
7 The journalist asked the pop star about his new album.
The pop star ______
8 A little girl in a pink dress gave the president a big bunch of flowers.
The president ______

2 VOCABULARY *-ed* / *-ing* adjectives

a Underline the correct adjectives to complete the sentences.

1 I watched a *fascinating* / *fascinated* documentary about tigers on TV last night.
2 I was so *boring* / *bored* during his lecture that I almost fell asleep.
3 That was one of the most *terrifying* / *terrified* horror movies I've ever seen.
4 I'm looking forward to doing nothing when I go on vacation next week. It's going to be so *relaxing* / *relaxed*.
5 The children were really *disappointing* / *disappointed* when Uncle Paul didn't bring them a present.
6 This cloudy, wet weather is so *depressing* / *depressed*. We haven't had sunshine in weeks!
7 I'm not really *interesting* / *interested* in modern art.
8 If you're not *satisfying* / *satisfied* with the service, you should complain.
9 Did you see Paola laughing during the professor's lecture? She looked very *amused* / *amusing*.
10 Our teacher told us we were probably going to get bad grades on his test. He wasn't very *motivating* / *motivated*. Now I really don't want to study.

3 PRONUNCIATION Sound and spelling: final *-ed* in adjectives

a 09.01 Listen to the sentences. Choose the sentence with the same *-ed* sound in **bold**.

1 He was fascinat**ed** by the movie trailer.
a ☐ She was inspir**ed** by the story of Greta Thunberg.
b ☑ They were disappoint**ed** with the quality of the food.
2 We were surpris**ed** by the violence in the movie.
a ☐ He felt depress**ed** after watching the environmental documentary.
b ☐ They were bor**ed** after watching only 15 minutes of the movie.
3 We listen**ed** to his jokes and were not amus**ed**.
a ☐ I was inspir**ed** to cook better after watching that TV show.
b ☐ My mom was shock**ed** by the news.
4 They were depress**ed** after they read the story.
a ☐ The students felt motivat**ed** when they left the classroom.
b ☐ She was embarrass**ed** by her boss.

9B I WENT TO A CONCERT THAT CHANGED MY LIFE

1 GRAMMAR Defining and non-defining relative clauses

a Rewrite the sentences. Use the information in parentheses as a non-defining relative clause.

1 The opera singer gave us some free tickets to her concert. (Her husband is a famous author.)
The opera singer, whose husband is a famous author, gave us some free tickets to her concert.

2 While you're in Italy, you should visit the town of Verona. (There is a beautiful Roman amphitheater in Verona.)
____

3 John Lennon was murdered in 1980. (He was a member of the pop group The Beatles.)
____

4 Pelé was a famous Brazilian soccer player. (His real name is Edson Arantes do Nascimento.)
____

5 Martin Scorsese was the director of the movie *The Departed*. (It was about the criminal gangs and corrupt police in Boston.)
____

6 First we went to Paris and then we took the train to Lyon. (In Paris, we visited the Eiffel Tower.)
____

7 In my opinion, Nirvana's best album is *Nevermind*. (They recorded it in 1991.)
____

8 Barack Obama is giving a talk at our university next month. (He was president of the U.S. from 2009 to 2017.)
____

2 VOCABULARY Music

a Complete the words in the text.

(1) When I was in London last summer, I went to an incredible concert at the BBC Proms, which is a [1]f*estival* of classical music at the Royal Albert Hall. It's great to hear a symphony or a concerto when it's [2]p__________ by an [3]o__________ of professional [4]m__________ who are playing [5]l__________. They played symphonies by Mahler and Beethoven, and there was also a huge [6]c__________ of 80 people that sang Mozart's Requiem. At the end of the concert, everyone in the [7]a__________ stood up and gave the performers a standing ovation, which lasted for over five minutes.

(2) I just heard on the radio that the band has been in the [8]r__________ studio for the last month. They're making a new [9]a__________ of jazz, soul, and blues songs, which is coming out in September. I just listened to an amazing [10]p__________ of their old songs on the Internet. It has about 30 [11]t__________ on it, and most of them are old songs of theirs from the '80s and '90s.

b 09.02 Listen and check.

3 VOCABULARY Word-building (nouns)

a Complete the sentences with the noun forms of the words in parentheses.

1 A lot of writers have tried to describe the *beauty* (beautiful) of the Taj Mahal in India.
2 My soccer team gave its best __________ (perform) of the season and won the game 4–0.
3 He has donated $100 to a __________ (charitable) that is providing schools for poor towns in Africa.
4 We believe that staff __________ (develop) is very important, so we provide regular training courses for all of our employees.
5 In my opinion, money can't buy you __________ (happy).
6 You need plenty of __________ (creative) to write good children's stories.
7 There will be a huge __________ (celebrate) downtown this New Year's Eve, with live performances by bands and a big fireworks display.
8 There is a fascinating exhibition of Aztec art and __________ (cultural) at the British Museum right now.

4 PRONUNCIATION Relative clauses: pausing

a 09.03 Listen to the sentences. Is the relative clause defining or non-defining? Check (✓) the correct box.

	Defining	Non-defining
1 … that have a lot of ads …	✓	
2 … which they recorded in 2010 …		
3 … whose brother is also a musician …		
4 … who eat healthily…		
5 … where I broke my foot …		
6 … that last more than three hours …		

9C EVERYDAY ENGLISH

It's supposed to be really good

1 USEFUL LANGUAGE

Recommending and responding

a Underline the correct words to complete the conversation.

ZOE Hi, Mel. Listen, Ian and I were thinking of [1]*go* / <u>*going*</u> out for dinner this weekend. [2]*Do* / *Would* you guys like to [3]*come* / *coming* with us?

MEL Yes, [4]*it's* / *that's* a great idea. Where were you planning [5]*going* / *to go*?

ZOE We [6]*think* / *thought* about going to that new Chinese restaurant in town. I [7]*was hearing* / *heard* it was really good.

MEL [8]*Hang* / *Wait* on a second. I'll ask Tony ... Sorry, Zoe, but Tony's not a big fan [9]*from* / *of* Chinese food.

ZOE OK, never mind. We could go somewhere [10]*other* / *else*.

MEL Oh, I know. How about [11]*go* / *going* to that new Italian restaurant by the movie theater?

ZOE Mmm, that [12]*seems* / *sounds* interesting.

MEL Yes, it's [13]*supposed* / *suggested* to be excellent, and a great value.

ZOE Yes, I'm sure Ian [14]*likes* / *would like* it. He loves pizza and pasta.

MEL Great! [15]*Should* / *Will* I book a table for Saturday evening?

ZOE Yes, that would be perfect for us. Why [16]*won't* / *don't* we get a table for 8 o'clock?

MEL Yes, OK. I'll book one.

b 09.04 Listen and check.

c Complete the words.

1 Sorry, but Sean's not a big f<u>an</u>____ of science fiction movies. What other movies are playing?
2 The new novel by J. K. Rowling, who wrote the Harry Potter books, is s__________ to be really good.
3 The new animated movie from Pixar has great r__________ in the papers.
4 **A** There's a documentary about the Roman occupation of Britain on TV tonight.
B Really? That s__________ interesting.
5 I'm not s__________ my father would be i__________ in going to an exhibition of surrealist paintings.
6 This hotel was r__________ by a friend of mine, who stayed here last year.
7 That's a great i__________. I'm sure Andy would l__________ it.
8 I h__________ the new Greek restaurant near my house w__________ really good.

d 09.05 Listen and check.

2 PRONUNCIATION

Showing contrast

a 09.06 Listen to the exchanges. Underline the word or words that are stressed in the responses.

1 **A** Did you go to the concert with Luke?
B No, I went with Will.
2 **A** Did James take the bus to Austin?
B No, he took the train.
3 **A** So your friend's a famous actor?
B No, she's a famous dancer.
4 **A** So you're from Lecce, in the south of Italy?
B No, I'm from Lecco, in the north of Italy.
5 **A** Are you meeting your friend Pam on Thursday?
B No, I'm meeting my friend Sam on Tuesday.

9D SKILLS FOR WRITING
I like going out, but ...

1 READING

a Read the blog and check (✓) the correct answer.

Mike likes watching sports on TV because ... .

a ☐ he can't see the players when he is at the stadium
b ☐ it's less expensive than going to the stadium
c ☐ it's dangerous to go to the stadium
d ☐ it's more exciting to watch the game at home

b Read the blog again. Are the sentences true or false?

1 Everyone in Mike's family likes watching their local team.
2 The sports channels that show live baseball games are free.
3 It is easier to see what is happening when you are at the stadium.
4 The TV commentator tells you a lot of interesting things about the players.
5 Mike doesn't like being in a huge stadium with thousands of other people.

Why I Prefer Watching Sports on TV
by Mike Adams

I love all kinds of sports, especially baseball, basketball, and tennis. However, I prefer watching it live on TV instead of going to the stadium.

The first reason for staying at home to watch sports is the cost. Although everyone in my family is a big fan of our local baseball team, I can't afford to pay for four tickets to watch a game at the stadium every two weeks. While I have to pay extra to get the sports channels that show live baseball games every week, it is much cheaper than going to the stadium.

Another reason I prefer watching sports live on TV is that you get a better view of the action. In a stadium, the spectators are not usually very close to the players, so it is sometimes difficult to see everything that happens clearly. Furthermore, on TV, they show you the action from a lot of different angles, and they replay the most important parts of the game again and again. And when you watch a game on TV, the commentator explains what is happening and gives you a lot of interesting information about the players and the teams, which you don't get when you're watching it at the stadium.

Finally, I don't enjoy being in a place where there are 50,000 other people. It's true that these days, baseball stadiums are very safe places to watch games. However, I sometimes get claustrophobic when I'm in a big crowd of people, so it's much better to be at home, where I can watch a game with my family or just a few friends.

So, although watching a game on TV probably isn't as exciting as being in the stadium, I generally prefer watching sports live on TV. It's cheaper, I can see the action more easily, and I can share the experience with my family and friends.

2 WRITING SKILLS Contrasting ideas

a Underline the correct words to complete the sentences.

1 I enjoyed seeing the new *Star Wars* movie at the movie theater, *although* / *in spite of* / *while* the noisy family who was sitting behind me.
2 *However* / *Despite* / *Although* I generally enjoy science fiction movies, I wouldn't recommend the film *Black Hole*.
3 Steven Spielberg is a great director. *However* / *While* / *Although*, I thought his last movie was actually pretty boring.
4 *However* / *Although* / *Despite* the loud rock music that accompanied most of the action scenes, I really enjoyed the movie.
5 *Despite* / *While* / *However* I agree with you that George Clooney is a good actor, I think he's mainly famous because of his looks.
6 *Although* / *Despite* / *However* it's more convenient to download movies from the Internet, more and more people are watching movies at their local movie theaters.
7 *Despite* / *While* / *Although* the superb acting and the exciting action scenes, I thought the movie was too long and kind of boring.
8 *While* / *However* / *In spite of* the amazing special effects, I wouldn't recommend that movie because the story wasn't very interesting.

3 WRITING

a Read the notes. Write an article explaining why you prefer reading the original book rather than watching a movie that has been adapted from a book.

Why I Prefer Reading a Book

Paragraph 1
- Introduction: State your position.

Paragraph 2
- Longer to read a book than watch a movie. More enjoyment from books.
- Interesting details often cut from movies.

Paragraph 3
- Need to use your imagination when reading a story.
- In movies, director decides appearance of people and places, not you.

Paragraph 4
- Books a great way to relax. Can enter a world that author created.
- Can read a book anywhere. Very convenient.

Paragraph 5
- Conclusion: Repeat the main points.

UNIT 9
Reading and listening extension

1 READING

a Read the text. Are the sentences true or false?

1 The main topic of the text is Marc Boulanger.
2 Marc Boulanger knows a lot about popular African music.
3 Marc Boulanger is from France.
4 Konono N°1 is the name of a music festival.
5 Tommo23 is interested in what Marc Boulanger wrote.
6 ShSh41 agrees with Marc Boulanger.

b Read the text again and check (✓) the correct answer.

1 Why was Konono N°1's concert so interesting to Marc?
a ☐ Fela Kuti had recommended the band to him.
b ☐ He had never visited Paris before.
c ☐ It was the first time he had ever heard popular African music.
d ☐ Their music was not similar to anything else he knew.

2 Who used to make traditional instruments out of elephant tusks?
a ☐ Fela Kuti
b ☐ Kanda Bongo Man
c ☐ People from Angola
d ☐ the Bazombo people

3 What is a *likembé*?
a ☐ a kind of elephant
b ☐ a kind of instrument
c ☐ a kind of musician
d ☐ a kind of sound

4 All the instruments used by Konono N°1 have been made by hand, … .
a ☐ apart from the instruments they found in the street
b ☐ except the electric instruments, which they bought
c ☐ including all the electric instruments that they use
d ☐ except for the piano and drums

5 According to ShSh41, who combined music with politics?
a ☐ Fela Kuti
b ☐ Kanda Bongo Man
c ☐ Konono N°1
d ☐ Mawangu Mingiedi

c You are going to write a blog for *Heroes of Music*. First, write notes about a singer, musician, or band whose music you like very much. Use the Internet to help you make notes about:

- the name of the singer/musician/band
- the history of the singer/musician/band
- any interesting details about the singer/musician/band.

HEROES OF MUSIC

Marc Boulanger, on the sweet sounds of Congolese band Konono N°1:

I was just 15 when I saw Konono N°1 perform live. They were playing a concert in Paris, my hometown, and although I had been serious about playing music since the age of 10, I had never seen or heard anything like this band before. I don't mean that I had never heard any popular African music before. Even at 15, I had already heard of musicians such as Fela Kuti and Kanda Bongo Man. So what was different about this folk orchestra?

First of all, I think it is the way that they mix modern culture with the cultural traditions of the Bazombo people, who live near the border with Angola. In that ancient tradition, musical instruments were made out of elephant tusks. But Mawangu Mingiedi, the musician who started Konono N°1, introduced electric *likembé* (a traditional *likembé* is part piano, part drum). They have a really special sound – they have a beauty that you just won't hear anywhere else.

Secondly, the instruments they use are really interesting. Every one of them has been made out of old bits of wood and metal and other trash that they have found just laying around. Even the electric instruments that they use have been made using batteries from old cars and broken lamps, as well as small magnets. Again, this all helps to create a sound that is unlike anything else you might hear.

Finally, there is the amazing rhythm they use. Every time I listen to it, I get a really strong feeling of excitement. Everyone who hears that beat is filled with so much happiness that they just have to start dancing.

COMMENTS

Posted by: Tommo23 09:13

Thanks for this. I just read Marc's full article. Really great story. They're going to do a performance at this year's Edinburgh festival in August. I can't wait to go.

Posted by: ShSh41 10:23

Yeah, I don't know. In spite of my love of African music, I think there are other bands that are more important than these guys. Fela Kuti is just the best. Now there was a guy who managed to put music and politics together. Definitely a hero for me.

2 LISTENING

a 09.07 Listen to three people talking and check (✓) the correct answers.

1 The speakers must be … .
   a ☐ at a local movie theater
   b ☐ at someone's house
   c ☐ in a classroom

2 The speakers are trying to decide … .
   a ☐ what to buy
   b ☐ what to eat
   c ☐ what to watch

3 Which type of movie do the women not want to watch?
   a ☐ comedy
   b ☐ documentary
   c ☐ science fiction

4 Which type of movie do they all agree to watch?
   a ☐ comedy
   b ☐ documentary
   c ☐ science fiction

b Listen again. Complete the sentences with the words you hear in the conversation.

1 The man says he remembered to order a *vegetarian* pizza.
2 They are going to watch the movies on the ________.
3 *Before the Flood* is the name of a ________ movie.
4 The man thinks the movie *Before the Flood* will probably be pretty ________ .
5 According to one of the women, the film *Man on the Moon* has amazing ________, beautiful photography, and a great story.
6 The man does not think that *Man on the Moon* is a ________.
7 The movie they all agree to watch is an ________ movie.

c Write about the kind of movies you like. Think about these questions:

- Do you think animated movies are only for children? Why / Why not?
- If you could direct a movie, what kind of movie would you most like to direct? Why?
- Which book would you most like to be made into a movie? Why?

Review and extension

1 GRAMMAR

Correct the sentences.

1 *Romeo and Juliet* is written from Shakespeare.
   Romeo and Juliet was written by Shakespeare.
2 A new bridge is built right now with a Chinese construction company.
3 I interviewed the actor which had just won an Oscar.
4 *Sunflowers* was painted from Vincent van Gogh.
5 Where the new James Bond movie being made?
6 He's the player used to be on our team.

2 VOCABULARY

Correct the sentences.

1 There was a fascinated documentary about the Antarctic on TV last night.
   There was a fascinating documentary about the Antarctic on TV last night.
2 The actor was annoyed because someone in the crowd had forgotten to turn off their cell phone.
3 My father's a professional music who plays the clarinet in the London Philharmonic Orchestra.
4 I loved the trailer, but the movie was pretty disappointed.
5 When I was about 16, I saw The Rolling Stones play life at a festival in Germany.
6 That director is so talented. Her movies always have such beauty photography.

3 WORDPOWER
see, look at, watch, hear, listen to

Correct the sentences. Use the correct form of the verbs *see*, *look (at)*, *watch*, *hear*, or *listen (to)*.

1 Why don't we see the game on TV at your house?
   Why don't we watch the game on TV at your house?
2 Have you watched my brother? He said he'd meet me here.
3 I don't hear why you're so angry with us.
4 She always hears pop music in her bedroom.
5 I'm looking at my grandparents next Sunday.
6 Sorry, the signal's terrible. I can't listen to you very well.
7 I finished this exercise. Please see it for me.

REVIEW YOUR PROGRESS

Look again at Review Your Progress on p. 114 of the Student's Book. How well can you do these things now?
3 = very well   2 = well   1 = not so well

I CAN …	
talk about movies and TV	☐
give extra information	☐
recommend and respond to recommendations	☐
write an article.	☐

10A IF I WERE IN BETTER SHAPE, I'D DO IT!

1 GRAMMAR Present and future unreal conditionals

a Complete the sentences with the correct forms of the verbs in parentheses. Use contractions where possible.

1 If you weren't (not be) so busy, you _____ (can) train to run a marathon.
2 I _____ (take) my daughter to the game if she _____ (be) interested in baseball.
3 I _____ (go) to the theater at least once a month if I _____ (live) in New York.
4 If I _____ (speak) Spanish, I _____ (apply) for a job in Madrid.
5 I'm sure you _____ (like) her if you _____ (know) her better.
6 I _____ (learn) another foreign language if I _____ (not have) so much work.
7 My sister _____ (buy) a new car if she _____ (can) afford it.
8 Germany doesn't have a very strong team at the moment, so I _____ (not be) surprised if England _____ (beat) them tomorrow.

b Decide if the present or future unreal conditional is more suitable for each situation. Complete the sentences using the correct form of the verbs in the box. Use contractions where possible.

be (x3) have not live visit come ~~pass~~ train pay not lose finish

1 You've studied really hard this year. If you pass your exams, I _____ for your vacation to Mexico.
2 He never goes to soccer training. If he _____ every day, he _____ a much better player.
3 Our team has won its last 10 games. If we _____ our next game, we _____ champions again.
4 My current salary's not very high. I _____ able to afford to buy a house if I _____ a job with a better salary.
5 Unfortunately, I live over 250 kilometers from my parents' house. If I _____ so far away, I _____ them more often.
6 I've done almost all my homework. I _____ and watch the game at your house if I _____ it before nine o'clock.

2 VOCABULARY Sports

a Underline the correct words to complete the sentences.

1 If your *competitor / opponent / referee* doesn't return the ball, you *miss / beat / score* a point.
2 No, I didn't enjoy the final. My team *lost / beat / missed* the game 2–0.
3 We *didn't win / didn't beat / didn't score* the game because you *lost / missed / attacked* that penalty shot.
4 The last time we played tennis together, I *won / lost / beat* you easily.
5 A standard running *court / net / track* has eight lanes, and each lap is 400 meters.

3 VOCABULARY Adjectives and prepositions

a Complete the sentences with one word from each box.

essential ~~proud~~ scared similar worried interested good

of (x2) for to in about at

1 That was the day my son won his gold medal. I was so proud of him.
2 Plenty of exercise and a good diet are _____ _____ a healthy lifestyle.
3 I'm not very _____ _____ current affairs.
4 I'm not very _____ _____ skiing. I love it, but I always fall over, and I have to go on the easiest slopes!
5 I think Portuguese is very _____ _____ Spanish.
6 My son hasn't studied enough, so he's really _____ _____ his exams.
7 She didn't want to go to the top of the Eiffel Tower because she was _____ _____ heights.

4 PRONUNCIATION Sentence stress: *would*

a 10.01 Listen to the pronunciation of *would* in these sentences. Is it strong (stressed) or weak (not stressed)? Write *S* (strong) or *W* (weak).

1 [W] I **would** go to the gym more often.
2 [ ] **A Would** he apply for a job in Canada?
[ ] **B** No, he **wouldn't**.
3 [ ] She **wouldn't** lend you any money.
4 [ ] You **wouldn't** enjoy that movie – it's too scary.
5 [ ] **A Would** you like to go get a pizza?
[ ] **B** Yes, I **would**.

10B MAKING THE MOST OF OPPORTUNITIES

1 GRAMMAR Past unreal conditionals

a Underline the correct words to complete the sentences.

1 She *had won* / *might have won* / *would win* the gold medal if she *hadn't fallen* / *didn't fall* / *wouldn't have fallen* at the start.
2 I *wouldn't have been able to* / *couldn't* / *hadn't been able to* get back into my house if *I would've lost* / *I've lost* / *I'd lost* my keys.
3 She *hadn't married* / *wouldn't have married* / *didn't marry* him if *she would've known* / *she knew* / *she'd known* that he'd been in prison.
4 If she *hadn't* / *wouldn't have* / *hasn't* helped him so much, he *might not have* / *hadn't* / *won't have* passed his exams.
5 We *hadn't* / *wouldn't have* / *won't have* gotten lost if you *hadn't* / *wouldn't have* / *had* forgotten to bring your phone.
6 If she *wouldn't read* / *didn't read* / *hadn't read* that letter, she *didn't find* / *wouldn't have found* / *hadn't found* out about her family in Russia.
7 They *would have won* / *had won* / *would win* the game if their captain *didn't miss* / *hadn't missed* / *wouldn't miss* that penalty shot!
8 If it *didn't start* / *hadn't started* / *wouldn't have started* raining, we *had finished* / *would finish* / *could have finished* our game of tennis.

b Complete the text with the past unreal conditional form of the verbs in parentheses. Use contractions where possible.

This is the story of how I met my wife, Jane. It all started when I was taking a taxi to work, and it suddenly broke down. If my taxi [1] hadn't broken (not/break) down, I [2] __________ (get) to the train station on time. If I [3] __________ (arrive) at the station on time, I [4] __________ (not/miss) my train. If I [5] __________ (not/miss) the train, I [6] __________ (not/have to) wait an hour for the next one. If I [7] __________ (not/have to) wait for an hour, I [8] __________ (not/go) to the café for a coffee. If I [9] __________ (not/got) a coffee, I [10] __________ (not/see) my friend Sarah – and if I [11] __________ (not/see) Sarah, she [12] __________ (not/introduce) me to her friend Jane. So Jane and I met because my taxi broke down that morning!

c 10.02 Listen and check.

2 VOCABULARY Expressions with *do*, *make*, and *take*

a Match 1–6 with a–f to make sentences.

1 [c] They've offered me a job in Paris, but I'm not sure if I want to take it or stay here. I have to make
2 [ ] If I had trained seriously over the past six months, I would have taken
3 [ ] I realize he's not a very sociable person, but please do
4 [ ] It's such a pretty day, so why don't we take
5 [ ] If we can wait a week and find the movie online, it doesn't make
6 [ ] His final exams are next month. If he does

a your best to persuade him to come to the party.
b advantage of the nice weather and go for a picnic by the river?
c a decision by the end of this week.
d sense for all five of us to go to the movies to see it.
e badly, he will have to repeat the whole year.
f part in last Sunday's marathon.

b Underline the correct words to complete the sentences.

1 José's a very outgoing and sociable boy, so I'm sure he'll *do* / *make* / *take* new friends easily when he starts his new school.
2 You've *made* / *done* / *taken* a lot of progress with your English over the past six months. Good job!
3 We've been driving for over two hours now. Let's stop at the next gas station and *make* / *do* / *take* a break.
4 We're *doing* / *making* / *taking* some research into our family history. It's amazing what we've discovered.
5 I *did* / *made* / *took* a big mistake and called my father-in-law "Tim" instead of "Tom." It was so embarrassing.
6 Who would *take* / *do* / *make* care of your grandmother if she were sick?
7 I've been *making* / *taking* / *doing* this math homework all night, and I still don't understand it.

3 PRONUNCIATION Sentence stress: *would* and *have*

a 10.03 Listen to the sentences. Underline the stressed words.

1 If I hadn't fallen over, I wouldn't have hurt my knee.
2 We wouldn't have missed the bus if you had gotten up on time.
3 Julia would have passed her exams if she had worked harder.
4 If they had saved some money each week, they might have had enough to buy a car.
5 She would never have married him if she had known about his first marriage.

10C EVERYDAY ENGLISH
You have nothing to worry about

1 USEFUL LANGUAGE
Talking about possible problems and reassuring someone

a Complete the conversation with the words in the box.

about feeling think worried nothing
happen it'll ~~feel~~ definitely what if

A How do you [1] _feel_ about the party tonight?
B Um, I'm [2] ________ OK …
A Good. Is everything ready?
B Yes, but I'm [3] ________ that not many people will come.
A You have [4] ________ to worry [5] ________. You've invited a lot of people.
B Yes, but [6] ________ only a few people come?
A That's [7] ________ not going to [8] ________. Everyone I've talked to says they're coming.
B Oh, good. Do you [9] ________ we'll run out of food?
A No, I'm sure [10] ________ be fine. You've made a lot of food, and most people will probably bring something.
B Oh, OK, that's good.

b 10.04 Listen and check.

c Put the words in the correct order to make sentences and questions.

1 what / that / start / time / the / me, / reminds / game / does ?
That reminds me, what time does the game start?
2 about / my / was / as / I'm / anyway, / worried / exam / saying, / I .
____
3 to / have / about / you / worry / nothing .
____
4 the Grammy Awards / music, / did / of / see / speaking / night / last / you ?
____
5 thinks / what / it's / if / everyone / boring ?
____
6 the / definitely / she's / like / going / ring / to .
____
7 go / afraid / something / will / that / wrong / I'm .
____
8 girlfriend / new / way, / have / by / you / the / his / met ?
____

d 10.05 Listen and check.

2 PRONUNCIATION
Sounding sure and unsure

a 10.06 Listen to the exchanges. Does speaker B sound sure (falling intonation) or unsure (rising intonation)? Write *S* (sure) or *U* (unsure).

1 **A** How much will an engagement ring cost?
B At least $1,000. [S]
2 **A** How long has your sister known her boyfriend?
B About four years. [ ]
3 **A** What time does the movie start?
B At quarter after eight. [ ]
4 **A** How often is there a train to Chicago?
B Every 45 minutes. [ ]
5 **A** How fast was the car going when the accident happened?
B About 100 kilometers an hour. [ ]
6 **A** How much does it cost to fly to New York?
B Around $600. [ ]

10D SKILLS FOR WRITING
I think you should go for it

Hi Carlos and Tom,

My bank has offered me the chance to go to Brazil! Apparently, we're going to open a new branch in Rio de Janeiro, and my manager has asked me if I'd like to go and work there. They would want me to stay for at least two years. I think it would be an amazing opportunity to live abroad and to get some experience working in a foreign country. It seems that they would provide me with free accommodation and pay for me to have Portuguese lessons. What do you guys think? Would it be good for my career if I worked in Brazil for two years?

Please let me know what you think.

Talk to you soon,

Brian

Hi Brian,

No wonder you sound so excited! Everyone says Rio is a fantastic place to live and that the Brazilians are such friendly people. I think you should definitely accept the offer. I'm pretty sure you'd enjoy living and working in Brazil and that you'd make a lot of new friends. Also, it would look good on your résumé if you worked abroad for a couple of years. And I'm sure it would be useful if you learned another language. So if I were you, I'd go for it.

Let me know what you decide to do.

Carlos

P.S. I'd definitely come to visit you on vacation!

Hi Brian,

I'm not sure what I think about the opportunity you've been given to spend two years in Brazil. I can see that it would be exciting to live in Rio, but if I were you, I'd think about it very carefully before making a decision.

I expect you'd have a great time in Rio, but you also need to think about your career with the bank. You've worked for your bank for over five years now, so maybe it would be better to apply for a management job either with them or with another bank in Florida? I'm not sure experience working at a bank in Brazil would help when you come back to look for a better job in Miami. I think you should discuss with your manager what kind of job your bank would give you if you came back after two years.

Let me know if you want to meet up to talk about it in more detail.

Best,

Tom

1 READING

a Read the emails and check (✓) the correct answer.

a ☐ Brian's not sure if he should accept the job in Rio.
b ☐ Brian has already accepted the offer of a job in Brazil.
c ☐ Brian wants to leave his bank and get a new job.
d ☐ Brian has decided not to accept the job in Rio.

b Read the emails again. Are the sentences true or false?

1. Brian's bank wants him to be the manager of their branch in Rio de Janeiro.
2. Brian wouldn't have to pay to rent an apartment or a house in Rio.
3. Carlos thinks that if Brian moves to Brazil, he'll probably feel lonely.
4. Carlos thinks it would be good for Brian's career to work in Brazil.
5. Tom doesn't think Brian would enjoy living in Rio.
6. Tom thinks working in Brazil for two years would definitely help Brian to get a better job in Miami.

2 WRITING SKILLS
Advising a course of action

a Complete the sentences with the words in the box.

should better definitely would
~~I'd~~ pretty expect suggesting

1. If I were you, ___*I'd*___ apply for that new job in marketing.
2. I'm not sure you ________ enjoy working for that company.
3. It would ________ be good for your career.
4. I'm ________ sure you'd be a good manager.
5. Maybe it would be ________ to try and get another job in Denver?
6. I ________ you'd find that training course extremely interesting.
7. I think you ________ definitely discuss it with your manager.
8. I'm just ________ that you think about it very carefully before you decide.

3 WRITING

a Read the email from Jane and write a reply. It can be positive and enthusiastic (in favor of her accepting the job) or more careful (advising her to consider going to college instead).

Hi!

I have some good news, but I also need some advice.

I just received my exam results and, fortunately, I passed all my classes and even got the honor roll in math and IT. As a result, I've been accepted to a great university to get a degree in business studies. However, the problem is that my parents don't think I should go to college. Although my dad didn't go to college, he's become a very successful businessman with a chain of small hotels around the country. Anyway, he wants me to start working as a trainee manager in one of these hotels. I worked there during the summer last year as a receptionist, and I really enjoyed it. So I'm thinking of accepting his offer of a permanent job now instead of going to college. Apparently, I could become a hotel manager within five years.

Please let me know what you think.
Thanks,
Jane

UNIT 10
Reading and listening extension

1 READING

a Read the email. Complete the sentences with the names in the box. You need to use some names more than once.

Alex Dean Luis Jack Pilar Robin Anthony

1 ___Dean___ wrote the email.
2 ________ received the email.
3 ________ and ________ are managers of local soccer teams.
4 ________ and ________ are soccer trainers.
5 ________ is the wife of one of the people in the email.

Hi Luis!

How are things in Madrid these days? How are Pilar and the kids?

Thanks for your last email and for your excellent advice about goalies. Your knowledge of soccer is just fantastic. Speaking of which, I need to ask your advice about something. So now that the team is taking a break from playing for a couple of months, I thought that this would be a good time to think about next year.

Generally, I was really proud of the players, but I think we were beaten too many times. I'm convinced that we would have won more games if we had attacked better. The defense is strong, but our attacking is just not that good. Although it's summer vacation, I've already told the team that they cannot take it easy.

First of all, they're just not in good enough shape, so they're all going to be doing more training. As I explained to them, "If you're going to take part in this beautiful game, then you are going to have to work much harder. I don't want you to do your best – I want you to win, win, and then win again." So from now on, they are going to do a good workout three times a week. Jack and Anthony (do you remember those guys?) are helping me do the training, so I know that they'll have to work really hard.

I also want to try changing the team. I don't think Alex or Robin should be on defense anymore. I think both of them will be good at playing up front because they are the only two who aren't scared of the ball (you should see the rest of them!).

Anyway, that's what I thought after watching the videos of this year's games. For instance, that game we played against the All Stars in March – I think if we'd had those two at the front, then we would have won easily. Can I ask you to take a look at the video (the link's below)? Tell me what you think. That reminds me – I saw the video of your team's last game, and I think you were right. If the referee had seen what number 7 had done to your goalie, there would have been a penalty for sure.

Well, I won't write any more. As you know, there's no time to relax when you're the manager of the local elementary school's ten-year-old girls' soccer team!

Best,

Dean

b Read the email again. Are the sentences true or false?

1 Dean respects Luis's knowledge of soccer.
2 Dean was mostly disappointed in the results of his team.
3 Dean thinks his team was most successful when they were attacking.
4 Dean has told his players that they are not allowed to have a rest.
5 Dean wants to reorganize his team.
6 Dean believes that most of his players try to avoid the ball during a game.
7 Dean agrees with Luis that the referee missed an important part of a recent game.
8 In general, Dean's email has been written in a formal style of English.

c Read the end of an email from Emily, your friend from Canada. Write a positive and enthusiastic reply to Emily's email. Think about the following:

- how to begin your email
- how to advise her on the best course of action
- ways of encouraging Emily to become the manager.

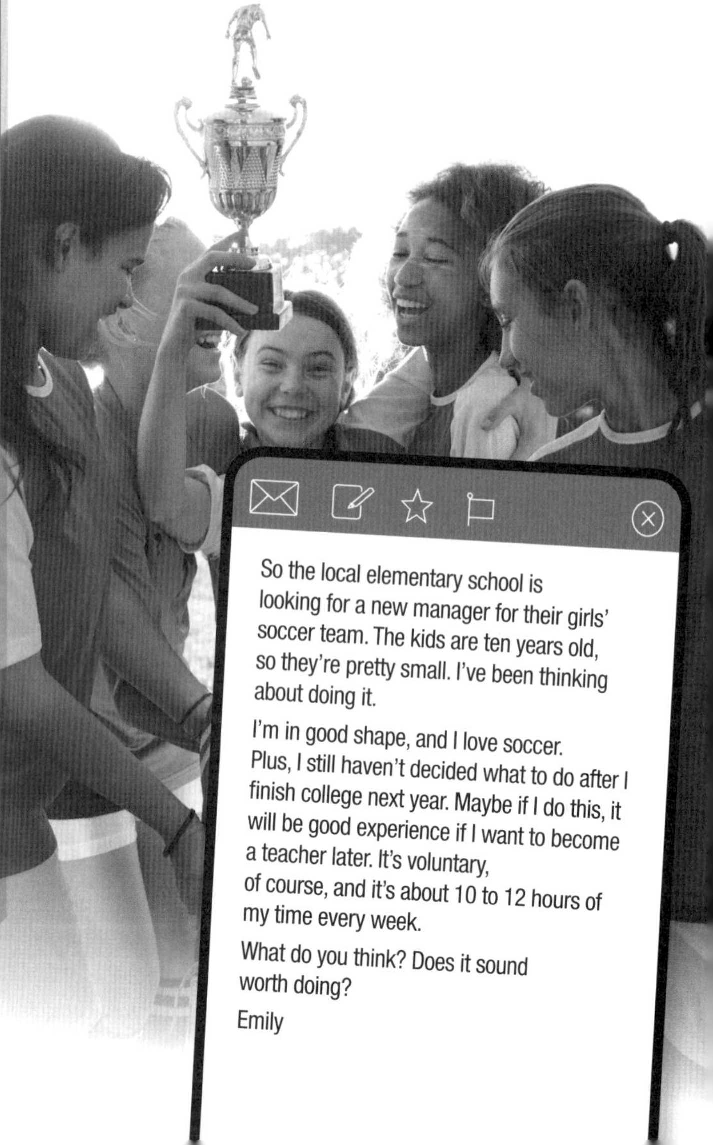

So the local elementary school is looking for a new manager for their girls' soccer team. The kids are ten years old, so they're pretty small. I've been thinking about doing it.

I'm in good shape, and I love soccer. Plus, I still haven't decided what to do after I finish college next year. Maybe if I do this, it will be good experience if I want to become a teacher later. It's voluntary, of course, and it's about 10 to 12 hours of my time every week.

What do you think? Does it sound worth doing?

Emily

2 LISTENING

a 10.07 Listen to a conversation between two students, Wendy and Pablo, and check (✓) the correct answers.

	Wendy	Pablo
1 Who seems to be unhappy?	☐	☐
2 Who had an interview recently?	☐	☐
3 Who wishes that they had gotten better grades at school?	☐	☐
4 Who describes a time when they felt very worried?	☐	☐
5 Who encourages the other?	☐	☐
6 Who needs some advice for a future interview?	☐	☐

b Listen to the conversation again. Check (✓) the correct answers.

1 According to Wendy, for every person accepted to medical school, how many people apply?
 a ☐ 2
 b ☐ 10
 c ☐ 12

2 Pablo reminds Wendy that she had excellent grades in … .
 a ☐ every subject
 b ☐ more subjects than Pablo
 c ☐ most subjects

3 When she describes her interview to Pablo, what does Wendy compare herself to?
 a ☐ an animal
 b ☐ her mother
 c ☐ the Sahara Desert

4 Pablo is sure that the people who interviewed Wendy … .
 a ☐ have all had a similar experience to Wendy's
 b ☐ must have understood how intelligent Wendy is
 c ☐ were all experienced and professional people

5 Wendy says that all doctors should be … .
 a ☐ confident
 b ☐ friendly
 c ☐ patient

6 Which of these things does Pablo suggest might help Wendy improve?
 a ☐ taking up a sport
 b ☐ finding a job in a theater
 c ☐ acting

c Choose a job from the box below. Write a conversation between two people. Person A has an interview for this job next week. Person B gives advice for the interview to Person A.

doctor engineer astronaut teacher salesperson

Review and extension

1 GRAMMAR

Correct the sentences.

1 If I would speak French, I would apply for that job in Paris.
 If I spoke French, I would apply for that job in Paris.
2 If there wasn't an accident, we didn't miss our flight.
3 If I were you, I will wait until the store has a sale to buy a jacket.
4 She didn't fail her exam if she studied harder.
5 If she would be nicer, she will make more friends.
6 We had caught the train on time if we left the house earlier.
7 I will buy a new car if I would have more money.
8 If it didn't rain yesterday, we would play tennis.

2 VOCABULARY

Correct the sentences.

1 The game finished 4–1 and Messi took three goals, including one penalty shot.
 The game finished 4–1 and Messi scored three goals, including one penalty shot.
2 I'm making some research into how children spend their pocket money.
3 In the final set, Roger Federer won Rafael Nadal 6–2.
4 I'm terribly sorry, miss, for doing a mistake with your check.
5 My cousin's really good in languages – she speaks German, French, and Russian.
6 Samantha's very worry about her exams.
7 He did a lot of money when he worked abroad, but now he's a teacher in Ohio.
8 We've been working for two hours now, so let's do a short break and get some coffee.

3 WORDPOWER Easily confused words

Underline the correct words to complete the sentences.

1 Can you *bring* / *take* these flowers to your grandmother's house, please?
2 That man *stole* / *robbed* my cell phone!
3 If we don't get to the station soon, we'll *lose* / *miss* our train.
4 In the summer, the sun *raises* / *rises* at 4:30 in the morning.
5 Can you *lend* / *borrow* me ten dollars, please?
6 He's *currently* / *actually* writing his third novel.

REVIEW YOUR PROGRESS

Look again at Review Your Progress on p. 126 of the Student's Book. How well can you do these things now?
3 = very well 2 = well 1 = not so well

I CAN …	
talk about new things it would be good to do	☐
talk about imagined past events	☐
talk about possible problems and reassure someone	☐
write an email with advice.	☐

AUDIOSCRIPTS

Unit 1

01.01

1 **A** Well, if you ask me, Rob Hernandez would be the best person for the job.
B Actually, I don't agree. As far as I'm concerned, Luke Adams would be better.

2 **A** Well, I guess you could take the shoes back to the store.
B I'm not so sure about that. I've already worn them.

3 **A** I think it's going to be difficult to make enough money to survive.
B Yes, I see where you're coming from. Maybe we should find a cheaper office?

4 **A** Well, in my opinion, Italian is easier than French.
B I know what you mean. I think it's easier to pronounce.

01.02

1 **A** It seems to me that their coffee is better than ours.
B Yes, I know exactly what you mean. It's really smooth, isn't it?

2 **A** As far as I'm concerned, I think it makes sense to take the train to Chicago.
B I'm not so sure about that. It takes almost three hours.

3 **A** I think France will probably win the World Cup.
B Yes, I think that's right. They have the best team.

4 **A** Well, in my opinion, we need to find another business partner in Latin America.
B Yes, I see where you're coming from. Maybe a company based in Ecuador this time?

01.03

1 **A** Guess what, Toni? I've just read about this girl, and she's only ten, but she's fluent in several different languages.
B That's fantastic. I can only speak one language – English.

2 **A** Hi, Marcela. Are you learning French?
B I'm trying to! But this book's useless! It teaches you how to say "my uncle's black pants," but not how to say "hello"!

01.04

NOAH So, Emily, are you going to tell me about your website? Are you working on it now?
EMILY Yes, it's almost ready, but I still have to finish some things.
N And who's it for?
E Well, you remember what I'm studying, don't you?
N Yes, uh, I think so. You're studying French or Spanish or something, aren't you?
E Well, kind of. I'm in the Latin American Studies department, so yes, I learn Spanish, but I also study history, culture, politics – all those kinds of things.
N Oh, right. So the website is for Latin American Studies students?
E Yes, but not just for them. It's also for Spanish students and for students from the World History department, too. They're all going to use it. And all the information on it has to be in Spanish, as well as English, so that I can keep in touch with all the students I met at UNAM.
N UNAM?
E Oh, that's the name of the university in Mexico where I was studying.
N Oh, I see. So are you writing everything in Spanish as well as English?
E Yes, I'm completely exhausted!
N I'm not surprised! That sounds like an absolutely enormous job!
E Well, I'm not doing everything on my own. There's a Colombian girl, Monica. She's helping me check my grammar and spelling and stuff.
N Oh, OK. So, what can I do to help?
E Well, I'm not very good at web design, so would you have any time to look at it for me? I need someone to check that everything on the website is working properly.
N Well, I'm a little busy …
E You have to help me, Noah! You're my only hope!
N OK, OK. I'll help you!
E Amazing! So, I've chosen the main photo for the website. But I thought maybe I could ask your opinion?
N Sure, let's have a look.
E Great. It's here on my phone.
N Wow! This is great! Where's this place?
E It's called Chichen Itza.
N Is that the name of the pyramid in the middle of the photo?
E No, Chichen Itza's the name of the ancient city. The pyramid … I can't remember what the name of the pyramid is.
N Well, anyway, it's a great photo for your website. It has history and culture, and it just looks really cool.
E Great! So when can you help me with the design of the website? Do you have any time …?

Unit 2

02.01

1 I applied for a lot of jobs.
2 We've worked very hard today.
3 I've learned a lot at this job.
4 They offered me more money.
5 You've had a fantastic career at CNN.

02.02

1 Could you ask your brother to help you?
2 Oh, really? That's terrible.
3 How about taking it back to the store where you bought it?
4 I'm really glad to hear that.
5 Why don't you try talking to your boss about it?
6 Let's take it to the garage.
7 Oh, no. How annoying!
8 Maybe you could try asking his girlfriend what kind of music he likes?

02.03

A I've lost my phone!
B Oh, no. How awful!
A I've been looking for it everywhere. I'm sure I had it when I got home.
B What about checking in your bag?
A OK … No, it's not in there …
B OK, so it's not in your bag. Have you tried calling it from another phone?
A That's a great idea. I'll give it a try. Could I borrow your phone for a minute?
B Yes, sure. Here you go.
A Oh, listen – it's ringing! It's behind that cushion on the sofa!
B Oh, that's great!

02.04

1 Veronica just bought a new car and it won't start!
2 My boss has been criticizing my work recently.
3 My neighbors had a party last night, so I didn't sleep very well.
4 My computer's been running very slowly since I installed that new program.

02.05

DIANE So, Carlos, how was your trip this morning? Did you drive or …?
CARLOS Oh, it was fine, thank you. I came by train from Philadelphia.
D I see. Right, well, let's start, shall we? To begin with, I'll ask you a few questions about your résumé, your education, your work experience, and so on. Then Steven is going to talk to you about the job. OK? Any questions so far?
C No, no, everything is fine so far, thank you.
D Great! OK, so can you tell me a little bit about yourself?
C Yes, of course. So, I'm 23 years old and I just recently completed a course in computer science at the University of Pennsylvania. And that was in Philadelphia, where I've been living for the last three, in fact, almost four years now. Before coming to the U.S., I went to school in Spain.
D Ah yes, that's right. I see from your résumé that you went to high school in Madrid.
C Yes, although I was actually born in San Francisco, in California. But when I was 14, I moved to Spain to live with my grandparents, who are from Madrid.
D Ah, so you speak Spanish, then?
C Yes, I do. In addition to English and Spanish, I also speak German. That's because of my father. He's an engineer from Düsseldorf.
D I see. That's very impressive. As you may already know, this company has offices in several different European countries, so we're eager to find people who can speak at least one other language as well as English.
C Well, that's good. I'd like the chance to use my languages.
D OK, now, in your opinion, why should this organization choose you for this job?
C That's a very good question. Well, first of all, I'm a people person. I'm very friendly and so I have a real ability to work on a team. Specialist knowledge is important, but you also need to be able to explain ideas simply and clearly. And that's something that I think I've learned at the job I do now. I think that experience will help me in this job.
D And why's that, may I ask? We don't really meet any customers with this job.
C True. But I soon learned that the best way to sell a phone wasn't to talk about all the technical things – it was to show people the apps! I discovered that I could sell more phones if I used clear and simple language to explain how to use them. So, for almost three years now, I've been staying up to date on all the most popular apps and selling more phones than anyone else.
D Very interesting. OK, now, …

Unit 3

03.01

1 Mark and Ali got to know each other when they worked in Ecuador.
2 They have a lot in common.
3 He gets along really well with his aunt.
4 I'm not very good at keeping in touch with old friends.
5 Most of my friends come from the same background.

03.02

1 The best thing is that my new apartment is air conditioned.
2 Anyway, we still hadn't found a hotel for my grandparents.
3 In the end, we bought him a video game.
4 It turned out that he had never played golf in his life.
5 You'll never guess what Sophia said to David.
6 The funny thing was that he didn't know she was joking.
7 You won't believe what he bought her for her birthday. A snake!
8 To make matters worse, the water was too cold to take a shower.

03.03

1 You'll never guess what happened at the party.
2 The best thing is that it has a swimming pool.
3 Anyway, we still had to find a present for Maria.
4 To make matters worse, it started raining heavily.

5 You won't believe what I did on Saturday.
6 The funny thing was that she didn't realize what had happened.
7 In the end, he agreed to drive us home.
8 It turned out that she had lost her train ticket.

03.04

1 But anyway, the train was still at the station, and we got on just as the doors were closing.
2 In the end, we went to a little restaurant near the station, where we had a wonderful dinner.
3 To make matters worse, the server dropped the tray of food, and it ruined my new white dress.
4 On top of that, when she eventually got to the airport, they told her that her flight was almost two hours late.
5 Anyway, in the end, I found a beautiful apartment downtown, and the best thing is that it's only a thousand dollars a month!

03.05

ROXANA Hi there! Hi, my name's Roxana Lara, and I'm a student here at the university. Do you have a few minutes?
BEN Oh, uh, sure. What do you need?
R Well, I'm taking a survey on family and friendship for my class, so would it be OK to ask you some questions?
B Sure. No problem.
R Great! Thank you so much! OK, so can you tell me your name and what you do?
B Sure. My name's Ben. Ben Boole. And I'm a second-year political science student.
R Well, hello Ben! Oh, I've said that already, haven't I? OK, so you're male – obviously – and your age group is 18 to 24?
B A little older, actually. I'm 28. So, you need to check the 25 to 32 box.
R Twenty-eight. Great, thanks. OK, so first question. Are you in a relationship?
B No, I'm single at the moment.
R No way!
B What?
R Nothing! Sorry – not married, no girlfriend – OK, next question! When you meet people for the first time, do you find it easy to make friends with them?
B Yes, I think so. I'm not shy. In fact, I think I'm generally pretty confident.
R OK, and how would you describe your childhood?
B Really happy. Um, I grew up in a pretty big family: there was my mom and dad, of course, but I also have five older sisters.
R Wow, so you're the youngest of six children, then?
B Yeah, that's right. But my grandparents also lived with us.
R So there were three generations and ten people living in the same house? Wow.
B Yes. Basically, I was brought up in a house full of women. My grandmother, my mom, and my older sisters. I think that's why I'm pretty confident now. I had so much support when I was growing up, I mean.
R How cool! OK, do you keep in touch with friends you made at school?
B Yes, I have a friend called "Zippy." Actually, his real name's Sipho, Sipho Zulu. His dad's from Zimbabwe. But everyone calls him Zippy.
R And did you get along with Zippy right away?
B No! Actually, that was the funny thing. Before we met, I was the best soccer player in the whole school.
R Oh, I'm sure you were.
B Sorry?
R Nothing.
B Uh, so anyway, Zippy was such a good player that I didn't really like him at first.
R So how did you become friends?
B Well, we eventually discovered that, although we come from different backgrounds, we had a lot of things in common. He's also the youngest child in a big family, and he also has older sisters. And we definitely have the same sense of humor.
R How important is a sense of humor in friendship?
B Oh, really important! I mean …

Unit 4

04.01

1 You don't eat meat anymore, do you?
2 It's a beautiful day today, isn't it?
3 Hugo's not going to ask her to marry him, is he?
4 You haven't been waiting long for me, have you?
5 She'd already bought him a present, hadn't she?
6 They'll call us when they get to the airport, won't they?
7 The twins both got good grades on their exams, didn't they?
8 Andrew speaks five languages fluently, doesn't he?
9 You don't want any rice, Jim, do you?

04.02

1 **A** Can you do something for me?
B Sure, how can I help you?
A Do you think you could cut the grass in my yard for me?
B Yes, of course. No problem.
2 **A** I've got a lot of things to get ready for the party tomorrow night.
B Is there something I can do?
A Yes, there is, actually. Can you give me a hand with the shopping?
B Yes, that's fine. Could I ask you a favor in return?
A Go ahead!
B Could you lend me your black pants for tomorrow?
A No problem. I'll go get them for you.
3 **A** Could I ask you a favor, Ben?
B Of course, what do you need?
A Could you help me move my desk into the other office?
B Actually, I have a bad back. Can you ask someone else?

04.03

1 You've been to Cairo before, haven't you?
2 Jack's really good at tennis, isn't he?
3 They have four children, don't they?
4 This is the best beach in Thailand, isn't it?
5 You're glad you left Dallas, aren't you?
6 You didn't go to Canada last year, did you?

04.04

Thank you, thank you. OK! So my talk tonight is called "Psychology in Advertising," but I'm going to start with a little story.
In the 18th century, Germany was divided into a lot of different countries. One of these was called Prussia, and the king there was called Frederick the Second. Now this particular king was a very talented man. In fact, he was so bright that he is still known as Frederick the Great.
OK, so at that time, the 1770s, hardly anyone in Prussia ate potatoes, because the main meal for almost everyone was bread. But there was a problem with bread: in those days, sometimes the wheat didn't grow very well, or it grew but then died before people could make bread from it. And every time that happened, people, especially poor people, would have nothing to eat.
So, when Frederick heard about the potato, he thought "A-ha! Perfect! If the people can eat these potatoes as well as bread, then no one will ever be hungry again!" Frederick was so satisfied with this idea that he immediately ordered everyone in the country to start growing potatoes. But to his surprise, they refused. They simply would not touch these potatoes. The people of Kolberg sent Frederick a letter telling him that potatoes were so disgusting that even their animals couldn't eat them.
Now Frederick was a very intelligent man, and although there were no psychologists in 1774, he certainly had a talent for understanding the psychology of his people. So, he soon came up with a very interesting plan.
First, he planted potatoes in a big field, which he called the "Royal Potato Garden." Next, because it was not just any potato garden, but the Royal Potato Garden, he sent soldiers to guard it.
As soon as people saw the garden and the soldiers, they started asking each other "What could be in that field that is worth so much?" And of course, as soon as they found out that the field was full of potatoes, they all wanted some. It was not long afterward that people started going to the field at night to steal potatoes. Frederick, of course, had expected this to happen. In fact, he had even given secret instructions to his soldiers to pretend that they had not seen the potato thieves and actually let them steal the potatoes, because that was what Frederick had wanted to happen.
There is an important lesson here for people about psychology in advertising.
When Frederick told people they would never be hungry again if they ate potatoes, they were not interested. When Frederick ordered them to grow potatoes, they refused. But when people believed that they were not allowed to eat potatoes, and that they were only eaten by kings and queens, then they immediately wanted to have them. And that's good psychology.

Unit 5

05.01

/eɪ/: save, danger, nature, education
/æ/: plant, dam, mammal, after, animal, branch, charity
/ə/: abroad, along, local, gorilla

05.02

1 If they offer me the job, I'm going to move to London.
2 We'll call you when our plane lands at JFK Airport.
3 If we don't stop hunting tigers, they'll be extinct in 20 years.
4 When the weather gets too cold, the birds fly south.
5 My dad will buy me a new laptop if I help him paint the house.
6 If you feel hungry later, have a banana or an apple.
7 I'll be there at 11 o'clock unless there's a problem with the train.
8 Unless the bus comes soon, I'm going to take a taxi.

05.03

1 Alicia doesn't enjoy her current job because she often has to work until 8 p.m.
2 There are a lot of things I can offer this company, like my talent for creating attractive websites and my experience of management.
3 It took me over an hour to get to work this morning due to a serious accident on the highway.
4 **A** There are some things I don't like about my job.
B Such as?
A Well, for instance, I don't like having to drive 50 kilometers to work every day.
5 Tom didn't get along with his new boss, so he decided to apply for a job at another company.
6 Since there weren't any meeting rooms free at 11 o'clock, they had to hold the meeting in his office.
7 I had to stay late at work yesterday. As a result, I didn't get home until nine o'clock.
8 My train arrived 45 minutes late this morning because of the bad weather in Chicago.

05.04

1 **A** So how old is your father now?
B Let me see. I think he'll be 62 in June.
2 **A** So what skills can you bring to this job?
B Well, to begin with, I have excellent project management skills.
3 **A** So why do you want to leave your current job?
B That's a good question. The main reason is that I need a new challenge.
4 **A** What time does their plane arrive at Heathrow Airport?
B Just a second. I'll check their email.

05.05

1 bore
2 pear
3 cap
4 bloom
5 cup

05.06

Thank you, thank you. So I'd like to begin today with something that the British writer Theodore Dalrymple once said.

Walking through the streets of the city where he lives, he starts to notice piles of trash everywhere he looks. And not just any trash, but the trash left behind by people who have bought food. And not just any food, but fast food, junk food.

Seeing all this, he asks himself: What did it mean? All this litter? At the very least, it suggested that an Englishman's street is his dining room ... as well as his trash can.

I wanted to share this with you because – well, partly because it is true, of course. Anyone who lives or has lived in a modern city will recognize that description – the streets of our cities are our dining rooms and our trash cans. But I have another reason for sharing that story with you, and that is that I want you to understand that pollution is not just something that happens to the natural environment or even to the wildlife that lives in it. It happens here, where we live. As I will explain during this talk, we cannot expect to improve the natural world if we do not first improve the condition of our own streets and cities. How can we expect to protect the environment from pollution when our own streets are full of trash?

In other words, we need to clean our own streets before we can even dream about preventing pollution in the rainforests of the Amazon, or the seas and oceans. And it is important to understand that the damage that we do to the world is not just "out there." It is here, and with us, all of the time. And we also need to remember that when we do damage to our environment, we are actually doing damage to ourselves.

So my talk today is called "Save yourself!" and my message is simple: we have to help ourselves before we can hope to help wildlife or the environment.

My talk is going to be in three parts. First of all, I will say some more about the problem of trash in the local areas where we live. It is now possible for us to manage our trash in a way that is environmentally friendly – but we don't. So in this part of my talk, I'm going to be asking "Why not? Why, when it is possible to be more environmentally friendly, do most people seem not to care?"

Next, I will discuss the problem of people. There are currently over seven billion of us in the world, and that is almost twice the number of people living in the world 50 years ago. For this reason, I will suggest that we need to change people's minds and I will also describe some ways of doing this. Ways that I think – I hope – will be successful in the future.

Finally, I will show how protecting your local area is the first step to protecting the planet for future generations of children.

Unit 6

06.01

PAUL I have my English exam tomorrow morning.
MOM That's right. So what time do you have to be at school?
P Well, the exam starts at 9 o'clock, so I can't be late.
M I think you ought to leave earlier than usual, in case there's a lot of traffic.
P Yes, that's a good idea.
M And what are you going to do after the exam?
P Well, I don't have to stay at school in the afternoon, so I can come home for lunch.
M Good, just two more things. It says on this information sheet that students must show their ID cards before the exam.
P Don't worry. I always take my ID card with me to school.
M It also says you can't use a dictionary during the exam, so don't take one with you.
P Yes, I know. I'll leave it at home.
M OK, good. By the way, it's 10 o'clock. You shouldn't go to bed late tonight.
P No, you're right. I'll go to bed now.
M OK, good night. And good luck for tomorrow!

06.02

1 guidebook
2 insect repellent
3 walking shoes
4 backpack
5 tour guide
6 culture shock

06.03

1 My lunch wasn't nearly as good as I expected.
2 This is by far the most luxurious hotel I've ever stayed in.
3 She plays tennis much better than I do.
4 Today's not nearly as hot as it was yesterday.
5 These are the most expensive shoes I've ever bought.
6 This restaurant is far cheaper than the restaurant we usually go to.
7 That was the hardest exam I've taken in my life.
8 Last night she got home earlier than usual.

06.04

1 He speaks more quickly than I do.
2 San Francisco is much more expensive than Chicago.
3 They make the best pizzas in Rome.
4 Colin is smarter than his brother.
5 That was the saddest movie I've ever seen.
6 The exam wasn't nearly as hard as I expected.
7 I think this is the simplest recipe in the book.
8 Right now, the weather in Turkey is a little warmer than in Spain.

06.05

A So where do you think I should take my mother on vacation?
B If I were you, I'd take her somewhere warm, like Italy.
A You've been to Italy lots of times, haven't you? Well, what would you recommend?
B Well, you should definitely go to Rome – it's such a beautiful city.
A That's a good idea. And when would you go?
B Hm, let me see. Well, you can't go wrong in May or June when it's not that hot. It's much better to go then than in July or August. Those months are too hot to go sightseeing.
A And where do you think we should stay in Rome?
B Well, there are some wonderful hotels downtown, but they're at least 200 dollars a night.
A You're kidding! I had no idea it would be that expensive. I can't afford to pay that much!
B Oh, well, in that case, it's probably worth finding a hotel outside downtown, then.
A Yes, that makes sense. Thanks for your advice.

06.06

1 You should definitely visit the British Museum when you're in London.
2 What dress would you wear to the party?
3 It's much better to take the train from Amsterdam to Paris.
4 It's probably worth booking a hotel before you go.
5 If I were you, I'd take the job in Portland.
6 Do you think I should buy this watch?

06.07

1 **A** My boyfriend's taking me to Paris this weekend!
B Wow! That's amazing.
2 **A** I've been accepted to Harvard University!
B Oh, really? That's good.
3 **A** I got the best exam grades in my class!
B That's amazing! Well done!
4 **A** My dad's going to buy me a rabbit!
B Wow! That's great.
5 **A** I got a promotion at work!
B Great! I'm so happy for you.
6 **A** We leave for vacation on Saturday!
B I know. I can't wait!

06.08

PEERAYA Hi Matt!
SILVIA Hi!
MATT Hi Peeraya, how are you doing?
P Really well, thank you! This is my friend Silvia, who I'm always talking about.
S Hi, Matt. Nice to finally meet you.
M Hi, Silvia.You too. So, what are you two up to?
P Well, you know I said in my text message that our English class is almost over.
M Yeah, right. It's gone really quickly, hasn't it?
P It really has. Anyway, we're planning to celebrate with a dinner out ...
S Yes, but, uh, we don't really know Boston very well.
P So ... we were kind of hoping you might be able to recommend some places to eat out?
S That would be really great.
M Yeah, sure. No problem at all. I mean, I'm not from Boston either, but I've lived here for a few years now, so I think I know it pretty well. Um, OK, so how many people is the dinner for?
S Oh, uh, 18 I think?
P Yes, well, there are 18 students in our class, but we'd like to invite our teachers, Molly and Sarah, too.
S Oh, yes, we definitely want them to come, too.
M OK, so that's dinner for 20 people?
S Yes. Oh, actually, no. I just remembered – Hiromi, one of the students, wants to bring her husband, Shigeru. So that would be 21.
M OK, so you'll need a fairly big restaurant then. There's nothing worse than waiting all night for one poor chef to try to prepare hundreds of appetizers and main courses.
P Yes, that's true!
S But also, we'd like to go to a place that's, uh, how do you say this in English? Um, we don't want to go to a big company place. You know, one of those places like *Star Noodles* or *Best Burgers* or any of those kind of places. We want to go to a, you know, something more like a family restaurant.
M Yes, I know what you mean. You don't want to go to any chain restaurants.
S That's right! No chain restaurants.
M Sure. OK, so places to eat out. Hmm. Well, you should definitely look at restaurants in West End. In fact, if I were you, I'd go to *The Thai House*. It's a really nice restaurant, and their seafood dishes are especially delicious. They're not too spicy, but the food is always really fresh there.
P That sounds nice. But we were thinking that this is an English class, so we'd like to go to a traditional American restaurant.
S Yes. I mean, do you know any places that do traditional American food, or even better, food from Boston?
M Ah! I see what you mean –
P But not ...
P/S Oysters!
M Don't worry! I knew what you meant. Well, it's probably worth going to *Bostonia Public House*. They do a really good clam chowder.
S I haven't tried clam chowder.
M It's very traditional here in Boston. It's a kind of thick soup with potatoes, onions, clams ... really tasty. You have to try it at least once.
P That sounds perfect!
S Yes, where is it?
M Well, do you know the traffic lights on the corner of State Street and McKinley Square?
P Yes.
M Well, you turn left there and go up State Street until you see an ATM. Turn left again and – you're there!
P Oh, thanks so much, Matt!
S Yes, thank you. That's great.
M No problem.

Unit 7

07.01

A Some new people have just moved into the house next door.
B Yes, I know. I saw them yesterday when they arrived. I think they're French.
A No, they can't be French. I heard them speaking a language that sounded like Spanish.
B Oh, really? They can't help me with my French homework, then.
A They could be Portuguese.
B That's true – Portuguese and Spanish sound alike.
A Is it a family or a couple?
B It must be a family. They must have two or three children.
A How do you know that?
B Because I saw some children's bikes in their yard. Also, there was another woman in the car when they arrived yesterday – she was older than the mother.
A She might be the children's grandmother.
B No, she can't be their grandmother. She looked too young.
A Or she could be their aunt? Or she might not be a relative at all. She may be just a friend. She might be helping them to unpack their things.
B Why don't we go and say 'hello'?
A But they might not speak English – it could be really embarrassing.
B They must speak English. I just saw them speaking to one of their neighbors, and they seemed to understand each other.

07.02

1 He must have rich parents.
2 She can't be studying for her exams tonight.
3 They might enjoy going to the zoo.
4 We must be pretty close to downtown now.
5 John must earn a lot more money than she does.

07.03

1 **A** Do you think you could help me with the shopping bags?
B Sure, I'll take them to the car for you.
2 **A** Is there anything I can do to help?
B Yes, there is, actually. Could you set the table for me?
3 **A** Do you think I could take a quick shower?
B Yes, of course. Let me get you a towel.
4 **A** May I use your phone?
B Yes, of course. Here you go.
5 **A** Do you mind if I watch the news on TV?
B Not at all. Let me turn it on for you.
6 **A** Would you mind taking your shoes off?
B No, not at all. Where should I leave them?

07.04

1 Would you mind opening that door for me?
2 Would you excuse me for a moment?
3 **A** Do you think I could have some coffee?
B Yes, of course. I'll make some for you.
4 **A** Would you mind if I used your bathroom?
B Not at all. Let me show you where it is.
5 Is there anything I can do to help?
6 Excuse me. Do you think you could turn the music down a little, please? It's really hard to talk in here.

07.05

1 **a** Would you mind getting me some more water?
b Would you mind getting me some more water?
2 **a** Do you think you could lend me some money?
b Do you think you could lend me some money?
3 **a** Can I make myself some coffee?
b Can I make myself some coffee?
4 **a** Do you think I could borrow your car?
b Do you think I could borrow your car?
5 **a** Do you mind if I make a quick phone call?
b Do you mind if I make a quick phone call?

07.06

LUIS OK, Ben, is it my turn yet?
BEN Um, not yet. You have to miss your turn this time because you only got three "ones," remember?
L Oh, yes, I forgot. So, whose turn is it now?
KATIA It's mine, yay!!! Come on, come on – be lucky! Give Katia the score she needs. OK, so I've got two "sixes." And what's that one? I can't see it from here.
B It's a "four."
K OK, so a "four" and two "sixes," sixteen. Is that good?
B Yes. You can move three places and you get – a "Dream" question.
K Ooh! Excellent! Go on.
B OK, "You have one minute to describe your dream home to the other players" – so just to Luis and Daniela, but not me. "Every player has to draw what you describe – but with their eyes closed!"
L/DANIELA What? / No! / I can't draw to save my life!
B Yes, yes. Just take a pencil and be quiet. OK, Katia? Close your eyes, Luis! Katia, are you ready? Good! So, one minute starting now!
K OK, so, my dream home! Let me see … oh, I know! I know! So, it would be in Paris, right downtown, in a fantastic location somewhere in a really nice neighborhood near to the Seine River. It would have to be on the top floor of a really big building so that I could see the river and even the Eiffel Tower from my window.
B What kind of building?
K A really big one.
B Yes, but what kind of building? Old? New?
K Oh, I see! OK, you're right, yes. Well, really new. Like from the 1990s or 2000s. In fact, from any time after 2010. So it would have a lot of shiny metal and glass on the outside and lots of gold and marble on the inside. Because, actually, my dream home isn't a house, but a luxury apartment. And it would be huge, I mean really, really big. And it would have a balcony along one side. The balcony would be really wide so that I'd have enough space for a lot of flowers and a garden and a table where I could have picnics and parties. Oh, and actually, it would also have a big, a really, really big, square dance floor.
B What about inside the apartment? They have to draw that too!
L Oh man, you're kidding, right?
B No, no. And close your eyes!
L Uff!
K OK, inside the apartment would be completely different from the building. It would be decorated just like a room in an Irish country cottage. So, there would be white walls and dark brown wood. And really old things. The kitchen would have an old metal oven where I could make cakes and bread and things. And I'd also …
B Time's up! OK, Picasso, let's have a look at, oh …

Unit 8

08.01

1 She doesn't know where the bathroom is, so she's going to ask the server.
2 Jack's parents don't usually allow him to come home after midnight, but he promised he would text them at 1 a.m. to let them know he was OK.
3 What beaches do you recommend visiting while we are in Florida?
4 Their neighbor threatened to call the police if they didn't turn down the music.
5 The radio warned us of the snow and traffic on the highway.
6 Casey didn't want to go to the concert, but his girlfriend persuaded him to go. He had a great time.

08.02

1 To be honest, the movie was kind of boring.
2 In my experience, Americans tend to be very friendly.
3 I don't generally like that kind of thing.
4 On the whole, I liked his new movie.
5 Some of his songs can be kind of depressing.
6 As a rule, Italian coffee is excellent.

08.03

1 He likes hip hop and rap music – you know, stuff like that.
2 We had a couple of days when it was cloudy and rainy, but on the whole we had pretty good weather.
3 Don't touch all that stuff in his office, please.
4 She likes watching documentaries about animals and nature and that sort of thing.

08.04

1 When did you last see her?
2 They went the wrong way and got lost.
3 Whose suitcase was the heaviest?
4 I wrote a long email to my uncle in Scotland.
5 I didn't know which book to get my husband.
6 She had to wait two hours for the next train to Portland.

08.05

/h/: whose, heaviest, husband, had
/w/: when, went, way, which
First letter silent: wrong, wrote, hours

08.06

KARINA Hi, Eva!
EVA Hi, Karina. How's it going?
K Well, I've had better days.
E Oh no, what happened?
K Well, do you remember those boots I was looking at last week?
E The brown leather ones?
K Yes. Well anyway, yesterday I decided to go back and buy them.
E Oh cool!
K Ah, well …
E Oh.
K Yes, "Oh." I thought they were a really good value when I bought them. I mean, fifty percent off a pair of designer boots that had just come out only six months ago?
E So what happened? Were they the wrong size or something?
K That's what typically happens to me but no, not this time. When I got home and took them out of the box, I realized why they were fifty percent off.
E What do you mean?
K As soon as I took them out of the box and turned them over, I saw that one of them had a big black mark on the side.
E That's absolutely awful. I hope you took them back to the store.
K Yes, of course I did, but …
E They didn't refuse to give you a refund, did they?
K Ha! Yes, you've got it! I couldn't believe it!
E I'm not surprised. But how …? I mean, what did they say?
K Well, I went back to the store, and I found the manager and told him what had happened, that I'd been to the store last week and tried on the boots, and then I'd gone back yesterday to buy them. I couldn't see them on the shelves, so I asked the assistant, and he brought them out already in the box.
E But didn't he show you the boots before you paid for them?
K Well, yes he did. He took the top off the box and asked me if everything was OK but by that time, you see, the boots were already lying flat inside the box. So I could only see the good side of them. I didn't think to ask him to take them out of the box again.

E Of course not. Why would you? So what did the manager say to that?
K He told me that as a rule they would always give someone a refund, but that that wasn't possible this time because they were on sale.
E You're kidding. So what happened?
K Well, he asked me if the sales assistant had shown me the boots in the box before I'd paid for them, and I admitted that he had. But I said that I hadn't realized that they were on sale because there was something wrong with them. But again, he just said that he was really sorry, but he couldn't give me a refund.
E Oh, what a …
K I know.
E So what's happening now?
K To be honest, I don't know. Jim suggested that I call a lawyer or something, but I'm not sure I want to go that far.
E Oh, I'm sorry. That really is bad, isn't it?
K I know, I know. So what would you recommend I do?
E Well, how about …

Unit 9

09.01

1 He was fascinated by the movie trailer.
She was inspired by the story of Greta Thunberg.
They were disappointed with the quality of the food.
2 We were surprised by the violence in the movie.
He felt depressed after watching the environmental documentary.
They were bored after watching only 15 minutes of the movie.
3 We listened to his jokes and were not amused.
I was inspired to cook better after watching that TV show.
My mom was shocked by the news.
4 They were depressed after they read the story.
The students felt motivated when they left the classroom.
She was embarrassed by her boss.

09.02

1
When I was in London last summer, I went to an incredible concert at the BBC Proms, which is a festival of classical music at the Royal Albert Hall. It's great to hear a symphony or a concerto when it's performed by an orchestra of professional musicians who are playing live. They played symphonies by Mahler and Beethoven, and there was also a huge choir of 80 people that sang Mozart's Requiem. At the end of the concert, everyone in the audience stood up and gave the performers a standing ovation, which lasted for over five minutes.
2
I've just heard on the radio that the band have been in the recording studio for the last month. They're making a new album of jazz, soul, and blues songs, which is coming out in September. I just listened to an amazing playlist of their old songs on the Internet. It has about 30 tracks on it, and most of them are old songs of theirs from the '80s and '90s.

09.03

1 Radio stations that have a lot of ads are really annoying.
2 The band's fourth album, which they recorded in 2010, was their best so far.
3 The pianist, whose brother is also a musician, gave an incredible performance.
4 In the article it says that people who eat healthily usually live longer.
5 Tickets for last year's festival, where I broke my foot, cost $250!
6 I think operas that last more than three hours are really boring.

09.04

ZOE Hi, Mel. Listen, Ian and I were thinking of going out for dinner this weekend. Would you guys like to come with us?
MEL Yes, that's a great idea. Where were you planning to go?
Z We thought about going to that new Chinese restaurant in town. I heard it was really good.
M Hang on a second. I'll ask Tony … Sorry, Zoe, but Tony's not a big fan of Chinese food.
Z OK, never mind. We could go somewhere else.
M Oh, I know. How about going to that new Italian restaurant by the movie theater?
Z Mmm, that sounds interesting.
M Yes, it's supposed to be excellent, and a great value.
Z Yes, I'm sure Ian would like it. He loves pizza and pasta.
M Great! Should I book a table for Saturday evening?
Z Yes, that would be perfect for us. Why don't we get a table for 8 o'clock?
M Yes, OK. I'll book one.

09.05

1 Sorry, but Sean's not a big fan of science fiction movies. What other movies are playing?
2 The new novel by J. K. Rowling, who wrote the Harry Potter books, is supposed to be really good.
3 The new animated movie from Pixar has great reviews in the papers.
4 **A** There's a documentary about the Roman occupation of Britain on TV tonight.
B Really? That sounds interesting.
5 I'm not sure my father would be interested in going to an exhibition of surrealist paintings.
6 This hotel was recommended by a friend of mine, who stayed here last year.
7 That's a great idea. I'm sure Andy would love it.
8 I heard the new Greek restaurant near my house was really good.

09.06

1 **A** Did you go to the concert with Luke?
B No, I went with Will.
2 **A** Did James take the bus to Austin?
B No, he took the train.
3 **A** So your friend's a famous actor?
B No, she's a famous dancer.
4 **A** So you're from Lecce, in the south of Italy?
B No, I'm from Lecco, in the north of Italy.
5 **A** Are you meeting your friend Pam on Thursday?
B No, I'm meeting my friend Sam on Tuesday.

09.07

DAVE OK, the pizzas are ordered.
MELISSA You remembered to get a vegetarian one for Diego and Kate, didn't you?
D Yes, yes. I got a vegetarian special. Oh, and there's plenty of soda for everyone, too.
M Great. OK, so what movie should we choose? This is supposed to be a movie night after all.
D Well, let's have a look. Can I turn on the TV?
M Yes, go ahead. I subscribe to the best movie sites, so we have a good variety to choose from. Do you want to take a look with me so we can pick something?
D Sure, thanks. OK, let's take a look. What's this, *Before the Flood*? Is that an action movie?
M Oh, no, it's a documentary. You haven't heard of it?
D Nope.
M Well, it's about climate change. It's with Leonardo DiCaprio – he meets with scientists and world leaders to talk about the dangers of what we're doing to the planet, and what we can do before it's too late.
D Oh, yeah?
M Yeah. It's an amazing movie.
D So you've seen it already?
M Yeah, but I don't mind seeing it again.
D Hmm. Sounds kind of serious, though. I mean I like documentaries, but I think it would be better to watch something fun. What do you think?
M Hmm, yes you have a good point. OK, well we don't have to watch that one. It was just an idea.
D Great. So what about a comedy? Are there any good ones?
LUCY Well, there's this one. It's pretty old now, but it has Jim Carrey in it and he's always been pretty funny, right?
D Jim Carrey?
L Yeah, you know, um … Well anyway, *Man on the Moon* is supposed to be really good. Amazing performances, beautiful photography, and a great story. I mean, it sounds really interesting and it was highly recommended by Professor Thomas.
D You mean your film studies professor?
L Yes, that's the one.
D Um, it sounds a little serious again. It says here that it's the biography of a comedian, but I'm not sure that it's actually a comedy. Yeah, look – most of the movie is about the problems he had and about how he had to deal with a terrible illness. I'm not a big fan of movies that are more intelligent than the audience, do you know what I mean? … You two really hate me now, don't you?
L No! Not yet.
M But I might in a minute if you don't choose a movie. Everyone will be here soon.
D OK, OK, just a moment. Hang on while I … There's *Avengers*.
M/L No!
M I'm not really a fan of science fiction. And neither is Maria, or Rachel, or …
L Or Diego or Kate. Or me.
D OK, OK. Wait a minute. Oh! Oh! I found it! I found it! This is the one!
L *Toy Story 4*? Isn't that a cartoon? And I haven't even seen the first three.
M It's supposed to be for kids, isn't it?
D Well, it is an animated movie, but it's not just for kids. It's a comedy. And it has some great songs. It's supposed to be really funny. It has great reviews!
M Well …
D It has great actors doing the voices. Tom Hanks …
M OK, then.
L Oh, OK. Hey, do you have cash to tip the pizza guy? Or do you need some more?
D I have it. I went to the bank earlier and …

Unit 10

10.01

1 I would go to the gym more often.
2 **A** Would he apply for a job in Canada?
B No, he wouldn't.
3 She wouldn't lend you any money.
4 You wouldn't enjoy that movie – it's too scary.
5 **A** Would you like to go get a pizza?
B Yes, I would.

10.02

This is the story of how I met my wife Jane. It all started when I was taking a taxi to work, and it suddenly broke down. If my taxi hadn't broken down, I would've gotten to the train station on time. If I'd arrived at the station on time, I wouldn't have missed my train. If I hadn't missed the train, I wouldn't have had to wait an hour for the next one. If I hadn't had to wait for an hour, I wouldn't have gone to the café for a coffee. If I hadn't gotten a coffee, I wouldn't have seen my friend Sarah – and if I hadn't seen Sarah, she wouldn't have introduced me to her friend Jane. So Jane and I met because my taxi broke down that morning!

10.03

1 If I hadn't fallen over, I wouldn't have hurt my knee.
2 We wouldn't have missed the bus if you had gotten up on time.
3 Julia would have passed her exams if she had worked harder.
4 If they had saved some money each week, they might have had enough to buy a car.
5 She would never have married him if she had known about his first marriage.

10.04

A How do you feel about the party tonight, then?
B Um, I'm feeling OK …
A Good. Is everything ready?
B Yes, but I'm worried that not many people will come.
A You've got nothing to worry about. You've invited a lot of people.
B Yes, but what if only a few people come?
A That's definitely not going to happen. Everyone I've talked to says they're coming.
B Oh, good. Do you think we'll run out of food?
A No, I'm sure it'll be fine. You've made a lot of food, and most people will probably bring something.
B Oh, OK, that's good.

10.05

1 That reminds me, what time does the game start?
2 Anyway, as I was saying, I'm worried about my exam.
3 You have nothing to worry about.
4 Speaking of music, did you see the Grammy Awards last night?
5 What if everyone thinks it's boring?
6 She's definitely going to like the ring.
7 I'm afraid that something will go wrong.
8 By the way, have you met his new girlfriend?

10.06

1 **A** How much will an engagement ring cost?
B At least $1,000.
2 **A** How long has your sister known her boyfriend?
B About four years.
3 **A** What time does the movie start?
B At quarter after eight.
4 **A** How often is there a train to Chicago?
B Every 45 minutes.
5 **A** How fast was the car going when the accident happened?
B About 100 kilometers an hour.
6 **A** How much does it cost to fly to New York?
B Around $600.

10.07

PABLO Hi, Wendy! How's it going?
WENDY Hi, Pablo. I'm doing OK. Not too bad.
P Hmm. You could try to sound more convincing when you say that!
W It's just … I had my interview this morning.
P Of course. How did it go?
W Awful. I want to be a doctor so much, but after that interview ...
P Oh come on, I'm sure it wasn't that bad. You've got nothing to worry about with your grades.
W Thanks, I know. But I'm pretty sure they want more than just good grades. I mean, this is medical school. I read somewhere that for every person accepted to medical school, at least 10 people apply. There are so many people who are expecting me to get accepted. What do I do if I don't? I'd be so embarrassed.
P But you didn't just get good grades. You got the highest grades at school in every subject. If only I had grades like yours. And I'm sure you did your best. You always do! So anyway, what happened at your interview that you seem to think went so badly?
W Well, I was so nervous I could hardly speak. I must have sounded like a mouse.
P But they're expecting people to be nervous. Who was interviewing you?
W Oh, it was two senior doctors from the hospital plus a second-year medical student who's in the program now.
P Well, OK, but remember they've all done the same interview once. They must have understood how you were feeling.
W I don't know. Maybe. I'm still convinced that I did something wrong. Doctors have to be really confident, don't they? I mean they have to tell people what to do, and they also have to make decisions that could mean life or death.
P Well, I guess …
W And you can't be nervous when you're talking to a patient. I mean, can you imagine? If you were my patient and you said "Oh, Doctor Wendy, do you think I'll be all right?" and then you heard me saying "Oh, um, well, uh, I, uh, think you'll, um, be fine!"
P You don't sound like that.
W But –
P Listen to me, Wendy – you don't sound like that. I promise you. And anyway, what's the worst thing that can happen? OK, let's just imagine that you don't get accepted to medical school this year –
W Oh!
P Just imagining! Anyway, what would you do?
W Um …
P OK, well I know what I'd do – I'd apply again next year, and I'd take advantage of the time off to do something really interesting. In fact, I'd do something that I knew would help me in my interview next year.
W Like what?
P Well, you say you need more confidence, right? Do some research. Find out what you could do that will help you become more confident. I don't know, like, you could try acting. Yes! What about that? You could get a job during the day and then in the evenings you could take part in a play or something. And don't forget, that would only be if you didn't get accepted to medical school, which you will, of course.
W Yeah, I suppose you're right. Thanks, that's really helpful. Actually, that reminds me, did you say there was something you wanted to ask me about?
P Ah, yes,I have an interview at the university's business school next week, and I wanted to ask you to give me some advice. I mean, I'm not sure what kind of questions they are going to ask me.
W Right, OK, well let's see …

ANSWER KEY

Unit 1

1A

1

a 2 hurts 3 happened 4 did they watch 5 did you talk 6 did he talk 7 got 8 did you vote

b 2 Which restaurant did your parents go to?
3 What happens to Will Smith at the end of the movie?
4 What did you and your friends talk about?
5 What was your first cell phone like?
6 What was his presentation about?
7 Which movie star got married twice last year?
8 Who did you go to the movies with?

2

a 2 into words 3 in touch 4 out 5 with 6 expressing 7 opinions

b 2 insisted 3 greeted 4 refused 5 encouraged 6 argue 7 persuaded 8 admitted

1B

1

a 2 d 3 h 4 e 5 f 6 b 7 a 8 c

b 2 Is she studying 3 's learning 4 Does she want 5 doesn't know 6 's 7 Does she play 8 loves 9 's 10 's playing 11 's ringing 12 's waiting

2

a 2 e 3 a 4 c 5 b 6 d 7 h 8 g

b 2 freezing 3 tiny 4 miserable 5 impossible 6 filthy 7 delicious 8 useless

1C

1

a 1 **B** concerned 2 **A** guess **B** sure 3 **A** think **B** see 4 **A** opinion **B** mean

c 1 **B** mean 2 **A** I'm concerned **B** sure 3 **A** think **B** right 4 **A** opinion **B** where

2

a 1 **A** Guess what, Toni? I've just read about this girl, and she's only ten, but she's fluent in several different languages.
B That's fantastic. I can only speak one language – English.
2 **A** Hi, Marcela. Are you learning French?
B I'm trying to! But this book's useless! It teaches you how to say "my uncle's black pants," but not how to say "hello"!

1D

1

a d

b True: 1, 4; False: 2, 3, 5

2

a 2 so that 3 This 4 This 5 in order 6 so

3

a **Suggested answer:**
How to Improve Your Cooking Skills

In order to become a good cook, the most important thing is to try new dishes and practice often. Most people usually cook the same dishes all the time. This means that they don't have the opportunity to improve their cooking skills by learning to cook new things.

It's a good idea to buy a few good recipe books so that you can learn how to cook some new dishes for the first time. At first, it's best to try cooking these new dishes for your family or only one or two close friends. This way you'll make sure that you can cook them successfully before you cook them for a larger group of people at a dinner party. To become a confident cook, you should try cooking new recipes two or three times a week. Why not ask your family or friends to tell you what they really think of your food so that you can make it better the next time?

Another good way to improve your cooking skills is to watch cooking shows on TV. It's usually easier to follow a recipe when someone shows you what to do. First, you can watch the TV chef, and then you can copy the recipe from the TV channel's website.

Finally, each time you enjoy a good dish at a friend's house or at a restaurant, don't be afraid to ask for the recipe. This is the best way to discover new dishes and to become a better cook.

Reading and listening extension

1

a True: 2, 3, 5; False: 1, 4

b 2 d 3 c 4 a 5 g 6 f 7 b

2

a 1 c 2 a 3 b 4 b

b 2 Latin American Studies 3 in Mexico 4 Another student 5 a city 6 absolutely perfect

Review and extension

1

2 My brother doesn't like coffee.
3 What was your vacation in Spain like? / How was your vacation in Spain?
4 Look at Tom – he's wearing his new shoes.
5 Who took you to the bus station?
6 Can you repeat that? I don't understand.

2

2 When we were young, my brother and I used to argue all the time, but now we've become good friends.
3 It's impossible to sleep because my neighbors are having a party.
4 I haven't gotten in touch with any of my old school friends in a while.
5 That cake was delicious, but there was only a tiny piece left!
6 I love that writer. She really knows how to put complicated feelings into words.

3

2 Help 3 Enjoy 4 teach 5 take care of 6 do

Unit 2

2A

1

a 1 **B** I've worked 2 **A** Have you ever arrived **B** I arrived 3 **A** Has she ever worked **B** she spent 4 **A** Matt's applied **B** hasn't had 5 **A** Have you met **B** I met

b 2 've worked 3 got 4 did you stay 5 stayed 6 did you like 7 enjoyed 8 gave 9 have you been 10 've been 11 have you had 12 joined 13 've been

2

a 2 c 3 b 4 f 5 h 6 a 7 d 8 g

b 2 charge 3 team 4 interview 5 résumé 6 experience 7 grades 8 apply

3

a 2 b 3 b 4 a 5 b

2B

1

a 2 've been waiting 3 's been posting 4 've been reading 5 's been cooking 6 Have, been crying 7 have been learning 8 has, been going

b 2 I've installed 3 turned off 4 hasn't been working 5 You've been playing 6 been waiting 7 I've had 8 We've been trying

2

a 2 password 3 off 4 app 5 share 6 deleted 7 click 8 upload 9 typing 10 username

b Across: 6 install 7 browser 8 type
Down: 1 upload 2 message 4 connect 5 delete

2C

1

a 2 terrible 3 taking 4 glad 5 talking 6 take 7 annoying 8 asking

c 2 What 3 worth 4 try 5 give 6 could 7 idea 8 let's 9 lose 10 Could

d 2, 10, 5, 9, 3, 7, 6, 1, 4, 8

2

a 2 My boss has been criticizing my work recently.
3 My neighbors had a party last night, so I didn't sleep very well.
4 My computer's been running very slowly since I installed that new program.

2D

1

a c

b True: 1, 3, 6; False: 2, 4, 5

2

a 2 e 3 a 4 c 5 b 6 d

3

a **Suggested answer:**

Hi Martina,

I'm sorry I haven't been in touch for the past few weeks but I've been incredibly busy.

I think I told you that I've been writing a story. I finished writing it a month ago and decided to send it to some publishing companies in New York. Well, you'll never believe this, but the editor of one of the biggest companies has just called to offer me a contract.

They want me to make a few changes to the story so that it is more interesting for young people. I'm going to work closely with one of their editors who will make suggestions for improving the story. Besides helping me to improve the novel, they're also going to pay me a lot of money. This means I can stop teaching and spend all of my time writing.

But the best thing is that they want me to go to California to meet some editors. I've never been to the West Coast before, so I'm really looking forward to it. What's really amazing is that they think my book could also become a movie. Apart from meeting their editors, they also want me to meet some movie producers in Hollywood!

What about having dinner together one day next week? There's a new Italian restaurant downtown that I'd like to try. Let me know a day that works for you.
Best,

Reading and listening extension

1

a 1 c 2 c 3 a 4 b

b 2 Dan 3 Neither 4 Kristen 5 Neither 6 Kristen 7 Dan 8 Neither 9 Kristen 10 Dan

2

a 7, 3, 5, 6, 2, 4, 1

b 2 a 3 c 4 b 5 a 6 b

Review and extension

1

2 I can't talk to Julia because she's been talking on the phone all day.
3 I went to Portugal on vacation three years ago.
4 I've known Jack for about five years.
5 His train was late this morning, so he just arrived.
6 Last night she went to the party with her sister.
7 He's been working as a taxi driver since 2008.
8 She has red eyes because she's been crying.

2

2 Please turn off your phones because the movie is about to start.
3 Can you give me your password so I can connect to the Internet?
4 I have a lot of experience managing people.
5 My brother just sent me a text message to say he'll be late.
6 Sarah applied for the job at the hospital, but she didn't get it.
7 The English keyboard is different from the one in my language, so I keep making mistakes when I type.
8 My brother just got a new job with a large bank in London.

3

2 for 3 up 4 forward 5 around 6 out

Unit 3

3A

1

a 1 had started, made
2 was cleaning, fell, broke
3 had stopped, was
4 rang, was having
5 met, was working
6 saw, looked, had escaped
7 were talking, arrived

b 1 were studying
2 left, had cycled
3 arrived, had escaped
4 rode, took
5 heard, was watching
6 crashed, were crossing
7 had closed, got
8 called, was waiting

2

a 2 c 3 e 4 a 5 b

b 2 friendship 3 old-fashioned 4 open-minded 5 calm 6 prejudiced

3

a 2 They have a lot in common.
3 He gets along really well with his aunt.
4 I'm not very good at keeping in touch with old friends.
5 Most of my friends come from the same background.

3B

1

a 2 usually walk
3 used to send
4 Did you used to get
5 didn't use to like
6 used to hang out
7 didn't use to have
8 Do you usually take

b 2 lives
3 used to drive
4 drives
5 used to go
6 goes
7 used to sit
8 sits
9 didn't use to eat
10 eats

2

a 2 e 3 g 4 b 5 a 6 h 7 d 8 c

3C

1

a 2 Anyway 3 end 4 turned 5 guess 6 funny 7 won't 8 matters

c 2 The best thing is that it has a swimming pool.
3 Anyway, we still had to find a present for Maria.
4 To make matters worse, it started raining heavily.
5 You won't believe what I did on Saturday.
6 The funny thing was that she didn't realize what had happened.
7 In the end, he agreed to drive us home.
8 It turned out that she had lost her train ticket.

2

a 2 In the end, we went to a little restaurant near the station, where we had a wonderful dinner.
3 To make matters worse, the server dropped the tray of food, and it ruined my new white dress.
4 On top of that, when she eventually got to the airport, they told her that her flight was almost two hours late.
5 Anyway, in the end, I found a beautiful apartment downtown, and the best thing is that it's only a thousand dollars a month!

b 2 In the end, we went to a little restaurant near the station where we had a wonderful meal.
3 To make matters worse, the server dropped the tray of food, and it ruined my new white dress.
4 On top of that, when she eventually got to the airport, they told her that her flight was almost two hours late.
5 Anyway, in the end, I found a beautiful apartment downtown, and the best thing is that it's only a thousand dollars a month!

3D

1

a c

b True: 1, 4; False: 2, 3, 5

2

a 2 b 3 a 4 e 5 d 6 c

3

a **Suggested answer:**

My grandpa's name was James Cooper, and my sister and I were very close to him. When we were children, we used to go to my grandparents' house every Sunday for lunch. Grandpa had a great sense of humor. He used to tell us a lot of jokes and funny stories about his travels around the world.

James Cooper was born in Burlington, Vermont, in 1938, and he had a very happy childhood. He had one brother and two sisters, and they all got along very well. In 1946, his family moved to Montreal, in Canada, and he lived there for 10 years. He grew up speaking English and French fluently, and in 1956, he returned to the U.S. to study medicine at Johns Hopkins University. He graduated in 1962 and worked as a doctor in different hospitals in Maryland from 1963 until 1972.

In 1972, he got a job at a hospital in San Francisco and lived in California for the next 13 years. While he was working there, he met Grandma, and they got married in 1974. One year later, my mother was born. They didn't have any other children, so she was an only child. When my mother was 10, Grandpa was offered a job in South Africa, and so they all went to live in South Africa in 1985. They lived there for five years, and they then returned to San Francisco in 1990. During their stay in Johannesburg, Grandpa became good friends with the famous South African heart surgeon Christiaan Barnard.

Grandpa retired in 1998 and died 12 years later, in 2010. We all miss him very much.

Reading and listening extension

1

a 1 b 2 c 3 b 4 a 5 c

b 4, 2, 7, 8, 1, 5, 6, 3

2

a True: 4, 5, 6, 7; False: 1, 2, 3, 8

b 1 c 2 b 3 c 4 b 5 b 6 b

Review and extension

1

2 I used to have long hair when I was a little girl.
3 He was playing basketball when he fell and hurt his ankle.
4 When he got to his house, he was angry because someone had broken his window.
5 I got to the train station five minutes late this morning and, unfortunately, my normal train had already left.
6 After the movie, we went to the café for coffee.
7 Did you use to play soccer when you were in school?
8 I didn't use to like English when I was in school.

2

2 Joanne's mother died when she was three, so she was brought up by her grandparents.
3 I got to know Jasmine really well when we went traveling around South America together.
4 All my relatives got together at my dad's birthday party.
5 I can't wait to hang out with my cousins at Thanksgiving.
6 She doesn't get along very well with her two brothers.
7 We have a lot in common, such as our love for literature.
8 My little brother's very calm and patient, so he takes after our mother because she's like that, too.

3

2 time 3 lunch 4 idea 5 look 6 bite

Unit 4

4A

1

a 2 Can you 3 he could 4 you'll be able to 5 was able to 6 couldn't 7 being able to 8 didn't manage to

b 2 f 3 d 4 c 5 a 6 e

2

a 2 ability 3 toward 4 determined 5 successful 6 gave up

b Across: 2 bright 4 confident 5 successful 6 determined 7 positive
Down: 1 ability 3 achievement 8 talented

4B

1

a 1 the, Ø 2 a, Ø 3 Ø, Ø 4 a, the 5 an, the 6 Ø 7 Ø, a 8 the, the

b 2 I usually go to the gym three times a week.
3 Is there a supermarket in front of the bus stop near your house?
4 She usually goes to school on the bus.
5 I often listen to the radio before I go to bed.
6 British pop groups are very popular in the U.S.
7 There isn't a subway station near my hotel, so I'll have to take a taxi.
8 Usain Bolt was the fastest man in the world at the Olympic Games in 2016.

2

a 2 outgoing/sociable 3 sensitive 4 shy 5 sociable/outgoing 6 talkative 7 reserved 8 serious

4C

1

a 2 e 3 f 4 c 5 g 6 d 7 b 8 a 9 i

2

a 1 **B** how **A** could 2 **B** something **A** hand **B** return
3 **A** favor **B** need **A** help **B** ask

3

a 2↘ 3↘ 4↗ 5↗ 6↘

4D

1

a 1 d 2 b

b True: 2, 4, 6; False: 1, 3, 5

2

a 2 h 3 f 4 b 5 a 6 c 7 e 8 d

3

a **Suggested answer:**

Summer camp coaches needed

Coaches are needed for a summer camp for children aged 5–12. Duties include organizing indoor and outdoor activities for the children, helping them get ready in the morning, helping during meals and at bedtime, and entertaining the children during their free time.

Candidates should be energetic and enthusiastic with an outgoing personality. A sense of adventure, a sense of humor, and a positive attitude are essential. Candidates should be good at sports and ideally have a talent for art. Our summer camp coaches should love working with children and should be able to get along well with all the other members of the team.

Candidates should be age 18 or over and preferably be college students or graduates. No previous experience is required. All new staff will be required to attend a two-day training course.

Candidates should complete the online application form and include an up-to-date résumé. You will be contacted by our Human Resources Department to discuss potential opportunities.

Reading and listening extension

1

a 1 a 2 b 3 c 4 c

b True: 1, 3, 5, 6; False: 2, 4, 7

2

a 1 b 2 b 3 c 4 c

b **Possible answers:**
2 Bread was the most important part of most people's diet.
3 Frederick thought that if people had potatoes, they would not be hungry anymore.
4 People in Kolberg said their animals could not eat potatoes.
5 People understood that potatoes were valuable when they saw the soldiers around Frederick's garden.
6 People began stealing potatoes from Frederick's garden.
7 Frederick's plan was successful.
8 Frederick's plan was an example of good psychology.

Review and extension

1

2 When she goes to the movies, she doesn't like seeing horror movies.
3 Will you be able to help me with my math homework tonight? / Can you help me with my math homework tonight?
4 I love watching documentaries about whales.
5 She would like to be able to play the piano as well as her sister.
6 He usually gets to work at about 8:30 in the summer.
7 We weren't able to find the restaurant, so we went to the pizzeria instead.
8 It's one of the best shopping websites on the Internet.

2

2 People really like Victor's sociable personality.
3 The Internet is surely one of man's greatest achievements of the last century.
4 My uncle was a very successful businessman in the 1960s.
5 Sandra is very intelligent. Did you know she can speak four languages?
6 José is so shy sometimes – he stands in the corner at parties and doesn't talk to anyone.

3

2 so far 3 or so 4 and so on 5 such 6 so tired

Unit 5

5A

1

a 2 g 3 a 4 b 5 h 6 e 7 d 8 c

b 1 **B** Yes, good idea. I'll call the pizzeria to book a table.
2 **A** What time is your brother arriving? / What time is your brother going to arrive? / What time will your brother arrive?
B This evening. I'll drive to the train station to meet him at 6:30. / I'm going to drive to the train station to meet him at 6:30.
3 Hello, John. The traffic's really bad downtown. We'll be about 20 minutes late. / We're going to be about 20 minutes late.
4 In my opinion, the next president of the U.S. will be a woman. / In my opinion, the next president of the U.S. is going to be a woman.
5 Can I help you bring in the groceries from the car?
6 **A** What time are you having your hair cut this afternoon? / What time are you going to have your hair cut this afternoon?
7 I don't think Brazil will win the soccer game tomorrow. / I don't think Brazil is going to win the soccer game tomorrow.
8 **B** I don't know. Perhaps he'll get a job at that new hotel at the beach. / Perhaps he's going to get a job at that new hotel at the beach.

2

a 2 e 3 d 4 c 5 b

b 2 climate 3 pollution 4 environmentally 5 destroyed 6 endangered 7 wildlife 8 conservation

3

a /eɪ/: save, danger, nature, education
/æ/: plant, dam, mammal, after, animal, branch, charity
/ə/: abroad, along, local, gorilla

5B

1

a 2 We'll call you when our plane lands at JFK Airport.
3 If we don't stop hunting tigers, they'll be extinct in 20 years.
4 When the weather gets too cold, the birds fly south.
5 My dad will buy me a new laptop if I help him paint the house.
6 If you feel hungry later, have a banana or an apple.
7 I'll be there at 11 o'clock unless there's a problem with the train.
8 Unless the bus comes soon, I'm going to take a taxi.

c 1 they'll be 2 see, invite 3 goes, changes 4 Unless, won't be able to 5 Open, feel 6 she misses, will have to 7 goes, usually feels 8 won't be able to, send

2

a 2 fur 3 paw 4 feathers 5 tail 6 petals 7 branches 8 web 9 scales

b Across: 4 oceans 6 desert 7 river 9 waterfalls
Down: 2 rainforest 3 lake 5 streams 8 cave

5C

1

a 2 like 3 due to 4 **B** Such as **A** for instance 5 so 6 Since 7 As a result 8 because of

2

a 2 Well 3 question 4 second

3

a 2 pear 3 cap 4 bloom 5 cup

5D

1

a 1 First of all 2 Secondly 3 Finally 4 In conclusion

b c

c True: 2, 3, 5; False: 1, 4

2

a **Suggested answer:**

Getting Our Energy From the Sun

If you think that you spend too much money on electricity, you might consider buying solar panels for your house. So, what are the advantages of solar panels?

Firstly, solar panels are a very efficient way of producing energy, and they are very good for the environment. They don't pollute the atmosphere with carbon dioxide or other harmful gases. If you live somewhere with plenty of sunshine, they will generate all the electricity you need for a family home.

Secondly, although they aren't cheap to buy or install, they will eventually save you a lot of money on your electricity bills. Also, if you produce more electricity than you need, your energy company will pay you for the extra electricity. As a result, you may earn extra money if you have solar panels.

Finally, solar panels can increase the value of your home. If your house has solar panels on the roof, people will usually pay a higher price because they know that they will save money on their electricity bills.

In conclusion, I would say that it is a very good idea to buy solar panels for your house. It is environmentally friendly, and it will give you cheaper electricity for many years.

Reading and listening extension

1

a A 4 B 5 C 6 D 3

b 1 b 2 a 3 b 4 b 5 c 6 a 7 a

2

a 3, 5, 2, 4, 1

b True: 2, 5, 6; False: 1, 3, 4

Review and extension

1

2 If he arrives before 2:00, we'll take him to that Italian restaurant for lunch.
3 Wait! I'll help you go shopping if you like.
4 Unless it rains this afternoon, we'll play golf.
5 I can't come with you because I'm playing basketball with Pablo this afternoon. We're meeting at the park at 3:00.
6 If they win the next game, they'll win the gold medal.

2

2 There are fantastic beaches on the coast near Rio de Janeiro.
3 It hardly ever rains in the desert.
4 Air pollution is a serious problem in big cities like Tokyo.
5 The leaves of that tree are as big as my hand.
6 She's working on a very important project to save endangered species from extinction.

3

2 fix 3 causes 4 tackle 5 are aware of 6 facing

Unit 6

6A

1

a 2 can't 3 ought to 4 don't have to 5 can 6 must 7 can't 8 shouldn't

c 2 b 3 a 4 e 5 d 6 c

2

a 2 d 3 f 4 b 5 a 6 e 7 h 8 g

3

a 2 <u>insect</u> repellent 3 <u>walking</u> shoes 4 <u>back</u>pack 5 <u>tour</u> guide 6 <u>culture</u> shock

6B

1

a 2 This is by far the most luxurious hotel I've ever stayed in. / This is the most luxurious hotel I've ever stayed in by far.
3 She plays tennis much better than I do.
4 Today's not nearly as hot as it was yesterday.
5 These are the most expensive shoes I've ever bought.
6 This restaurant is far cheaper than the restaurant we usually go to. / The restaurant we usually go to is far cheaper than this restaurant.
7 That was the hardest exam I've taken in my life.
8 Last night she got home earlier than usual. / She got home earlier than usual last night.

c 2 San Francisco is much more expensive than Chicago.
3 They make the best pizzas in Rome.
4 Colin is smarter than his brother.
5 That was the saddest movie I've ever seen.
6 The exam wasn't nearly as hard as I expected.
7 I think this is the simplest recipe in the book.
8 Right now, the weather in Turkey is a little warmer than in Spain.

2

a 2 cooked 3 raw 4 crunchy 5 creamy 6 sour 7 fresh 8 heavy

b 2 mash 3 chop, fry 4 Add 5 mix, serve 6 Heat up, stir

6C

1

a 2 were 3 recommend 4 definitely 5 would 6 wrong 7 better 8 should 9 kidding 10 worth

c 2 wear 3 to take 4 booking 5 I'd 6 should

2

a 2 bored 3 excited 4 excited 5 bored 6 excited

6D

1

a 1 A 2 B 3 A 4 A

b True: 1, 5, 6; False: 2, 3, 4

2

a 2 slightly 3 a little 4 fairly small 5 extremely 6 completely 7 reasonably 8 extremely

3

a **Suggested answer:**

Last Saturday I took my girlfriend to *Chez Pierre* for her birthday. It's a new French restaurant downtown. The atmosphere was really relaxing, and although there was classical and French music, it wasn't very loud, so it was easy to talk. The servers were extremely friendly, and the service was good. Our fish was absolutely delicious, and the salad was very fresh and tasty. For dessert, I had a lovely apple tart with cream, and Anna had ice cream. All the portions were extremely generous, and although the meal was fairly expensive, I would definitely recommend going there for a special occasion.

A friend of mine recommended the *Villa Borghese* restaurant to us. It's an Italian restaurant near the beach, and they serve mostly Italian food such as pizza and pasta. Unfortunately, it was a little disappointing. The restaurant was extremely noisy because there were a lot of young children and loud pop music, so it was fairly difficult to talk. Because of this, the atmosphere wasn't very relaxing. We went on a Friday evening, and the restaurant was completely full, but there weren't enough servers. The service was awful – we were there for nearly an hour before anyone took our order. We ordered pasta, but it was slightly overcooked, and the sauce wasn't very tasty. Our meal was fairly cheap, but the food wasn't very good, so I definitely wouldn't go there again.

Reading and listening extension

1

a True: 1, 4; False: 2, 3

b 1 a 2 b 3 c 4 b 5 a 6 c

2

a 1 c 2 b 3 a 4 a

b 2 for a fairly long time 3 21 4 chain 5 traditional American dishes 6 soup 7 turn left

Review and extension

1

2 I think this is the best Greek restaurant in New York.
3 Last night we had to take a taxi because we missed the bus.
4 His house is closer to the university than yours.
5 You must not park outside that school.
6 He's taller than his older brother.
7 You must not feed the animals in the zoo – it's forbidden.
8 I think Spanish is easier to learn than English.

2

2 Can I borrow your spoon so I can stir my coffee?
3 She said we should read the guidebook to avoid a lot of culture shock.
4 You need to chop the onion and garlic before you put it in the pan.
5 Squeeze the lemon and pour the juice over the fish.
6 If you put in too much sugar, it will be too sweet to drink.

3

2 f 3 c 4 b 5 a 6 e

Unit 7

7A

1

a 2 e 3 a 4 c 5 f 6 d 7 b

b 2 can't 3 could 4 must 5 must 6 might 7 can't 8 could 9 might not 10 may 11 might 12 might not 13 could 14 must

2

a Across: 3 neighborhood 5 doorbell 7 lock 8 balcony
Down: 2 location 4 basement 6 floor

b 2 rented, apartment 3 landing, floor 4 front, locks 5 out of, into 6 balcony, view

3

a Final /t/: 4, 5

7B

1

a 1 some 2 enough 3 too many 4 plenty 5 a few 6 no 7 enough 8 little

b 2 Unfortunately, there aren't any good restaurants near here. / Unfortunately, there are no good restaurants near here.
3 He won't pass his exams because he hasn't worked hard enough this year.
4 **A** Is there any milk left? / Is there much milk left?
B Yes, we've got plenty.
5 There were too many people at the bus stop to get on the bus.
6 There are too few eggs in the fridge to make an omelet. / There aren't enough eggs in the fridge to make an omelet.
7 My father's too old to play tennis these days.
8 She made a lot of mistakes in her translation. / She made lots of mistakes in her translation.

2

a 2 about 3 for 4 about 5 on 6 about 7 with 8 in

b 2 cope with 3 apologized to 4 rely on 5 worried about 6 belongs to 7 complained about 8 argued with

7C

1

a 2 f 3 e 4 c 5 a 6 b

c 2 control 3 Sure 4 thank you 5 great 6 Let

d 2 excuse 3 **A** I could **B** I'll 4 **A** I used **B** Let 5 anything 6 could

2

a 2 b 3 b 4 a 5 a

7D

1

a c

b True: 3, 4; False: 1, 2, 5

2

a 2 There's a good store at the end of my street. Alternatively / Otherwise / Apart from that, you could go to the huge supermarket, which is just before you get to the highway.
There's a good store at the end of my street. Another option / Another possibility is to go to the huge supermarket which is just before you get to the highway.
3 You can get a good view of London from the London Eye. Alternatively / Otherwise / Apart from that, you can go to the top of The Shard building.
You can get a good view of London from the London Eye. Another option / Another possibility is to go to the top of The Shard building.
4 I suggest you go to the beach early in the morning, before it gets too hot. Alternatively / Otherwise / Apart from that, you could go late in the afternoon.
I suggest you go to the beach early in the morning, before it gets too hot. Another option / Another possibility is to go late in the afternoon.
5 Why don't you go to that Italian restaurant next to Washington High School? Alternatively / Otherwise / Apart from that, you could try that new Japanese restaurant near the new supermarket.
Why don't you go to that Italian restaurant next to Washington High School? Another option / Another possibility is to try that new Japanese restaurant near the new supermarket.

3

a **Suggested answer:**

Hi Pascale,

Thanks for babysitting for us this evening. Hope you get along well with the children and that everything goes well. Here are some suggestions for the evening.

Please make yourself at home and help yourself to something to drink and eat. There is some tea and coffee by the fridge. Otherwise, you can make some hot chocolate. It's in the cupboard to the right of the fridge. There are plenty of chocolate cookies on the table. Alternatively, there's some delicious cheesecake in the fridge.

Can you give the children their dinner at around 7 o'clock? In the fridge, there's some tomato soup and chicken nuggets. You can heat it all in the microwave. Another option is to make them some sandwiches. You'll find plenty of cheese in the fridge, and there's also some apple juice.

After that, you could watch something on TV with them. They both love watching *Spongebob Squarepants*. Otherwise you could watch one of their favorite movies with them, such as *Toy Story 4* or *Finding Nemo*.

By the way, they usually go to bed at about 9 o'clock. You can read them a bedtime story. You'll find plenty of books on the bookcase in their bedroom. They both love the *Harry Potter* books. Another possibility is to start reading *The Lion, the Witch and the Wardrobe* with them. I think they might enjoy it.

Finally, if you have any problems, please call me on my cell phone: (614) 555-3192. Alternatively, you can call my husband's/wife's cell phone: (614) 555-3871.

Hope you have a good evening and see you around 11:30.

Reading and listening extension

1

a A 6 B 1 C 5 D 3

b 9, 7, 8, 2, 3, 1, 6, 4, 10, 5

2

a 2 f 3 a 4 e 5 c 6 d

b 1 c 2 c 3 c 4 c 5 a 6 c 7 b 8 c

Review and extension

1

2 George isn't good enough at soccer to play for the school team.
3 She can't be the manager – she looks too young!
4 There's a lot of traffic / There's lots of traffic downtown during rush hour.
5 They can't be doing their homework right now – it's almost midnight!
6 The math exam was too difficult for most of the people in my class.

2

2 She complained to the server about the dirty glass.
3 I can't afford to buy an apartment right now, so I'm going to rent an apartment downtown.
4 Don't worry about the check. I'll pay for the meal.
5 I live in a really nice neighborhood – everyone's very friendly.
6 When he told me about the accident, I didn't believe him at first.

3

2 c 3 a 4 f 5 e 6 d

Unit 8

8A

1

a 2 She said I should wait behind the line until it was my turn.
3 When I talked to her last Friday, she asked me if I was going to the meeting that afternoon.
4 She told me (that) he might be about 50 years old.
5 He told me he was sorry but he couldn't find my post on Facebook. / He said he was sorry but he couldn't find my post on Facebook.
6 She asked me if I had seen my uncle when I was in New York last month. / She asked me whether I had seen my uncle when I was in New York last month. / She asked me if I had seen my uncle when I was in New York the month before. / She asked me whether I had seen my uncle when I was in New York the month before.
7 He told Anna he would see her next week. / He told Anna he would see her the following week.

b 2 He said that Martin had just sent him a text.
3 He told me he would call me when he got home from work.
4 He asked me if I was going to send my brother an email that afternoon. / He asked me whether I was going to send my brother an email that afternoon.
5 She asked me why I couldn't lend her some money.
6 The teacher said that we needed to stop writing immediately and give him / her our papers.
7 She told me she wanted me to take the flowers to my grandmother.

2

a 2 brainstorm 3 sent 4 sent 5 have 6 putting up 7 listened to 8 hold

b Across: 1 episode 5 updated 7 call 8 series
Down: 2 poster 3 delivered 4 subscribe 6 newsfeed

8B

1

a 1 going 2 seeing 3 to get 4 to come 5 visiting 6 waiting
7 going, to see 8 paying

b 2 Don't forget to give me back my book when you finish reading it.
3 He admitted to stealing the woman's bag.
4 We hoped to find a good place to eat on one of the streets near the train station.
5 He threatened to tell my parents what I had done.
6 It's really important to teach your children how to cross the street safely.
7 She didn't know which book to buy her brother for his birthday.
8 You promised to help me with my homework!

2

a 2 agreed 3 suggested 4 warned 5 refused 6 offered

b 2 promised 3 recommend 4 threatened 5 warned 6 persuaded

8C

1

a 2 In my experience, Americans tend to be very friendly.
3 I don't generally like that kind of thing.
4 On the whole, I liked his new movie.
5 Some of his songs can be kind of depressing.
6 As a rule, Italian coffee is excellent.

2

a 2 couple, whole 3 stuff 4 sort

3

a /h/: whose, heaviest, husband, had
/w/: when, went, way, which
First letter silent: wrong, wrote, hours

8D

1

a d

b True: 1, 4; False: 2, 3, 5

2

a 2 I heard a story on the radio about an elephant that, apparently, sat on a car in a safari park.
3 The 12-year-old girl took her father's motorcycle and rode it for 40 km on the highway before the police stopped her near Milwaukee. / The 12-year-old girl took her father's motorcycle and rode it for 40 km on the highway, but the police stopped her near Milwaukee.
4 The woman hit the teenager hard on his head with her umbrella and then used his cell phone to call the police. / The woman hit the teenager hard on his head with her umbrella before using his cell phone to call the police. / The woman hit the teenager hard on his head with her umbrella and then called the police with his cell phone. / The woman hit the teenager hard on his head with her umbrella before calling the police with his cell phone.
5 Amanda escaped from the burning building by breaking a window with her shoe.
6 There was an incredible story on the news about a baby in China who fell from a fourth-floor window, but she wasn't hurt because a man in the street caught her.

3

a **Suggested answer:**

There was an incredible story on the Internet today about a car that crashed into a family's house in Manchester. Apparently, Richard and Judy Knowles and their children were watching TV when suddenly they heard a loud noise. The driver had lost control of his car and had driven straight through the front door of the house before stopping two meters from the kitchen. Amazingly, no one in the house or in the car was seriously hurt. It seems that the family of four and their dog were all in the living room at the time of the accident. When they realized what had happened, they immediately called the police, who arrived at the scene five minutes later. The front of the house was badly damaged but, fortunately, the driver of the car and his three passengers only suffered minor injuries. It took the firefighters six hours to remove the vehicle from the house.

Reading and listening extension

1

a 1 c 2 c 3 b 4 b

b 2 Shanna 3 Neither 4 Shanna 5 Neither 6 Shanna 7 Mercedes 8 Shanna 9 Neither 10 Mercedes 11 Shanna 12 Mercedes

2

a True: 2, 3, 4, 7; False: 1, 5, 6, 8

b 1 b 2 a 3 a 4 b 5 c 6 b

Review and extension

1

2 They asked me if I was going to the soccer game. / They asked me whether I was going to the soccer game.
3 He has agreed to take us to the airport.
4 When I called him last night, he said he had just finished his exams.
5 She advised me not to tell anyone about our meeting.
6 Yesterday, he said he would help me with my homework. / Yesterday, he told me he would help me with my homework.
7 I'm really looking forward to seeing you on Sunday.

2

2 I suggest sending a text before you call her.
3 Do you have time to have a chat later today?
4 He advised me to buy a new laptop because mine is over five years old.
5 I subscribed to that podcast because I liked the name.
6 She promised us that she would send an email when she arrived.
7 We ought to brainstorm some ideas this morning.

3

2 on 3 on 4 in 5 in 6 on 7 in 8 in

Unit 9

9A

1

a 2 The movie *Ready Player One* was directed by Steven Spielberg.
3 The actors have been told to come back at 3 p.m.
4 1,000 movies are made in Bollywood every year.
5 The movie *Avatar* was seen by 35 million people in its first two weeks.
6 The president is being interviewed on TV right now. / The president is being interviewed right now on TV.
7 200,000 cars are produced by our new factory every year. / 200,000 cars are produced every year by our new factory.
8 This old house is being used in the movie.

b 2 Five different varieties of orange are grown in this region.
3 Students will be given a loan to pay for their college tuition by the government. / Students will be given a loan by the government to pay for their college tuition.
4 The special effects are being created with the latest animation software.
5 The actors have been asked to give some of their money to charity.
6 The car was being driven really fast when the accident happened.
7 The pop star was asked about his new album by the journalist. / The pop star was asked by the journalist about his new album.
8 The president was given a big bunch of flowers by a little girl in a pink dress.

2

a 2 bored 3 terrifying 4 relaxing 5 disappointed 6 depressing
7 interested 8 satisfied 9 amused 10 motivating

3

a 2 b 3 a 4 b

9B

1

a 2 While you're in Italy, you should visit the town of Verona, where there is a beautiful Roman amphitheater.
3 John Lennon, who was a member of the pop group The Beatles, was murdered in 1980.
4 Pelé, whose real name is Edson Arantes do Nascimento, was a famous Brazilian soccer player.
5 Martin Scorsese was the director of the movie *The Departed*, which was about the criminal gangs and corrupt police in Boston.
6 First we went to Paris, where we visited the Eiffel Tower, and then we took the train to Lyon.
7 In my opinion, Nirvana's best album is *Nevermind*, which they recorded in 1991.
8 Barack Obama, who was president of the U.S. from 2009 to 2017, is giving a talk at our university next month.

2

a 2 performed 3 orchestra 4 musicians 5 live 6 choir 7 audience
8 recording 9 album 10 playlist 11 tracks

3

a 2 performance 3 charity 4 development 5 happiness 6 creativity
7 celebration 8 culture

4

a 2 non-defining 3 non-defining 4 defining 5 non-defining 6 defining

9C

1

a 2 Would 3 come 4 that's 5 to go 6 thought 7 heard 8 Hang 9 of
10 else 11 going 12 sounds 13 supposed 14 would like 15 Should
16 don't

c 2 supposed 3 reviews 4 **B** sounds 5 sure, interested 6 recommended
7 idea, love 8 heard, was

2

a 1 No, I went with <u>Will</u>.
2 No, he took the <u>train</u>.
3 No, she's a famous <u>dancer</u>.
4 No, I'm from <u>Lecco</u>, in the <u>north</u> of Italy.
5 No, I'm meeting my friend <u>Sam</u> on <u>Tuesday</u>.

9D

1

a b

b True: 1, 4, 5; False: 2, 3

2

a 2 Although 3 However 4 Despite 5 While 6 Although 7 Despite
8 In spite of

3

a **Suggested answer:**

Why I Prefer Reading a Book

I love going to the movies, and I have seen a lot of movies that are based on famous books. However, I normally prefer reading the original book to seeing the movie version.

The first reason for enjoying the book more than the movie is because a book usually takes several days or weeks to read, whereas a movie only lasts for two or three hours. So I can enjoy reading a book for much longer than watching a movie. Furthermore, because most movies are much shorter than books, the director has to cut a lot of the interesting details from the story. As a result, movies only show the most important scenes of the story and don't usually tell the audience what the characters are thinking.

Another reason I prefer the book is that when you are reading a story, you have to use your imagination. The reader imagines what the people and the places in the story look like and how the characters speak. However, this isn't possible when you watch a movie because the director makes the decisions about the appearance of the characters and the scenes.

Finally, reading a book is a great way to relax and to enter the world that the author has created. You can read a book anywhere you like – in bed, on the beach, or on a bus as you travel to work. While it is true that these days you don't have to watch a movie at the movie theater or on TV, it is still much easier to take a book with you and read a chapter when you have nothing else to do for half an hour.

So, although it is much easier to watch the movie adaptation of a novel than to read the original book, I prefer reading the book. It lasts longer and gives me more enjoyment, it allows me to use my imagination, and it is a very good way to relax.

Reading and listening extension

1

a True: 2, 3, 5; False: 1, 4, 6

b 1 d 2 d 3 b 4 c 5 a

2

a 1 b 2 c 3 c 4 a

b 2 TV 3 documentary 4 serious 5 performances 6 comedy
7 animated

Review and extension

1

2 A new bridge is being built right now by a Chinese construction company.
3 I interviewed the actor who had just won an Oscar.
4 *Sunflowers* was painted by Vincent van Gogh.
5 Where is the new James Bond movie being made?
6 He's the player who used to be on our team.

2

2 The actor was annoyed because someone in the audience had forgotten to turn off their cell phone.
3 My father's a professional musician who plays the clarinet in the London Philharmonic Orchestra.
4 I loved the trailer, but the movie was pretty disappointing.
5 When I was about 16, I saw The Rolling Stones play live at a festival in Germany.
6 That director is so talented. Her movies always have such beautiful photography.

3

2 Have you seen my brother? He said he'd meet me here.
3 I don't see why you're so angry with us.
4 She always listens to pop music in her bedroom.
5 I'm seeing my grandparents next Sunday.
6 Sorry, the signal's terrible. I can't hear you very well.
7 I finished this exercise. Please look at it for me.

Unit 10

10A

1

a 1 'd be able to / could 2 'd take, were 3 'd go, lived 4 spoke, 'd apply 5 'd like, knew 6 'd learn, didn't have 7 would buy, could / were able to 8 wouldn't be, beat

b 1 'll pay 2 trained, 'd be 3 don't lose, 'll be 4 'd be, had 5 didn't live, 'd visit 6 'll come, finish

2

a 1 score 2 lost 3 didn't win, missed 4 beat 5 track

3

a 2 essential for 3 interested in 4 good at 5 similar to 6 worried about 7 scared of

4

a 2 **A** W **B** S 3 S 4 S 5 **A** W **B** S

10B

1

a 1 hadn't fallen
2 wouldn't have been able to, I'd lost
3 wouldn't have married, she'd known
4 hadn't, might not have
5 wouldn't have, hadn't
6 hadn't read, wouldn't have found
7 would have won, hadn't missed
8 hadn't started, could have finished

b 2 would've gotten / would have gotten 3 'd arrived 4 wouldn't have missed 5 hadn't missed 6 wouldn't have had to 7 hadn't had to 8 wouldn't have gone 9 hadn't gotten 10 wouldn't have seen 11 hadn't seen 12 wouldn't have introduced

2

a 2 f 3 a 4 b 5 d 6 e

b 2 made 3 take 4 doing 5 made 6 take 7 doing

3

a 1 If I hadn't fallen over, I wouldn't have hurt my knee.
2 We wouldn't have missed the bus if you had gotten up on time.
3 Julia would have passed her exams if she had worked harder.
4 If they had saved some money each week, they might have had enough to buy a car.
5 She would never have married him if she had known about his first marriage.

10C

1

a 2 feeling 3 worried 4 nothing 5 about 6 what if 7 definitely 8 happen 9 think 10 it'll

c 2 Anyway, as I was saying, I'm worried about my exam.
3 You have nothing to worry about.
4 Speaking of music, did you see the Grammy Awards last night?
5 What if everyone thinks it's boring?
6 She's definitely going to like the ring.
7 I'm afraid that something will go wrong.
8 By the way, have you met his new girlfriend?

2

a 2 U 3 U 4 S 5 U 6 S

10D

1

a a

b True: 2, 4; False: 1, 3, 5, 6

2

a 2 would 3 definitely 4 pretty 5 better 6 expect 7 should 8 suggesting

3

a **Suggested answer:**

Positive reply:

Hi Jane,

That's great news about your exams! Congratulations!

I think you should definitely accept your dad's offer of a job. I'm pretty sure you'd enjoy working in one of his hotels as a trainee manager. You'd probably become a hotel manager in a few years, and that would be fantastic. Also, I think it would be better to take a job now instead of going to college for a degree. It might be hard to find a job when you finish. I think this could be an excellent opportunity for you, so if I were you, I'd go for it.

Let me know what you decide to do.

Talk soon,

Careful reply:

Hi Jane,

That's great news about your exams! Congratulations!

I'm not sure what I think about your dad's offer. I can see that it would be exciting to train as a hotel manager but, if I were you, I'd think about it very carefully before making a decision.

I expect you'd enjoy working in one of your dad's hotels, but you also need to think about your career. Maybe it would be better to go to college and get a degree before you start working in a permanent job? If you get a degree in business studies, you'll be able to apply for jobs in a lot of different areas of business after you graduate. On the other hand, if you start working in the hotel industry now, you might find that it's hard to get into another area in the future. I'm just suggesting that it might be better to go to college first and then decide what you want to do after you graduate.

Let me know if you want to meet up and talk about it.

Talk soon,

Reading and listening extension

1

a 2 Luis 3 Dean, Luis 4 Anthony, Jack 5 Pilar

b True: 1, 4, 5, 6, 7; False: 2, 3, 8

2

a 1 Wendy 2 Wendy 3 Pablo 4 Wendy 5 Pablo 6 Pablo

b 1 b 2 a 3 a 4 a 5 a 6 c

Review and extension

1

2 If there hadn't been an accident, we wouldn't have missed our flight.
3 If I were you, I'd wait until the store has a sale to buy a jacket.
4 She wouldn't have failed her exam if she had studied harder.
5 If she were nicer, she'd make more friends.
6 We would have caught the train on time if we had left the house earlier.
7 I'd buy a new car if I had more money.
8 If it hadn't rained yesterday, we would have played tennis.

2

2 I'm doing some research into how children spend their pocket money.
3 In the final set Roger Federer beat Rafael Nadal 6–2.
4 I'm terribly sorry, miss, for making a mistake with your check.
5 My cousin's really good at languages – she speaks German, French, and Russian.
6 Samantha's very worried about her exams.
7 He made a lot of money when he worked abroad, but now he's a teacher in Ohio.
8 We've been working for two hours now, so let's take / have a short break and get some coffee.

3

2 stole 3 miss 4 rises 5 lend 6 currently

Acknowledgments

The authors and publishers acknowledge the following sources of copyright material and are grateful for the permissions granted. While every effort has been made, it has not always been possible to identify the sources of all the material used, or to trace all copyright holders. If any omissions are brought to our notice, we will be happy to include the appropriate acknowledgments on reprinting and in the next update to the digital edition, as applicable.

Key
U = Unit.

Photographs
The following photographs are sourced from Getty Images.

Front cover photography by Thomas Barwick/DigitalVision.

U1: Tim Pannell; Westend61; Antonio_Diaz/iStock/Getty Images Plus; Johanes Minawan Laksana/iStock/Getty Images Plus; Julian Love/Cultura; DragonImages/iStock/Getty Images Plus; Lane Oatey/Blue Jean Images/Collection Mix: Subjects/Getty Images Plus; Cinoby/iStock/Getty Images Plus; **U2:** Skynesher/E+; PeopleImages/E+; Dougal Waters/DigitalVision; Bymuratdeniz/E+; Fizkes/iStock/Getty Images Plus; izusek/E+; Ariel Skelley/DigitalVision; **U3:** XiXinXing; Ascent/PKS Media Inc./Stone; Nopphon Pattanasri/EyeEm; Tom Werner/DigitalVision; Fanjianhua/iStock/Getty Images Plus; Jenny Cundy/Cultura; Sshepard/E+; **U4:** Tomwang112/iStock Getty Images Plus; SolStock/Moment; Michaeljung/iStock/Getty Images Plus; Ziga Plahutar/E+; Miroslav_1/iStock/Getty Images Plus; **U5:** Spondylolithesis/iStock; Eli_asenova/E+; Pawel Libera/The Image Bank; Jeffbergen/E+; Bruce Leighty/Photolibrary/Getty Images Plus; Miles Willis/Getty Images News; Narvikk/E+; David Trood/DigitalVision; **U6:** Andria Hautamaki/Moment; Fizkes/iStock/Getty Images Plus; Eoneren/E+; Coward_lion/iStock Editorial/Getty Images Plus; Roberto Soncin Gerometta/Lonely Planet Images/Getty Images Plus; Adamkaz/E+; **U7:** Kali9/E+; Tom Werner/DigitalVision; SolStock/E+; Andresr/E+; Mapodile/E+; Bill Swindaman/Moment; John Henley/Corbis/Getty Images Plus; **U8:** Morsa Images/E+; Luis Alvarez/DigitalVision; Compassionate Eye Foundation/Mark Langridge/DigitalVision; Yellow Dog Productions/The Image Bank; Jacobs Stock Photography Ltd/DigitalVision; Anna Summa/The Image Bank/Getty Images Plus; Monkeybusinessimages/iStock/Getty Images Plus; Tim Robberts/DigitalVision; Carol_Anne/iStock/Getty Images Plus; **U9:** Rowan Jordan/E+; Danita Delimont/Gallo Images/Getty Images Plus; David Aaron Troy/The Image Bank/Getty Images Plus; FilippoBacci/E+; Fug4s/iStock/Getty Images Plus; Ariel Skelley/DigitalVision; Christian Brecheis/Corbis/Getty Images Plus; Rouzes/E+; **U10:** Hendrik Sulaiman/EyeEm; Sol de Zuasnabar Brebbia/Moment; Pekic/E+; Chris Howes/Canopy/Getty Images Plus; Alistair Berg/DigitalVision.

The following photographs are sourced from other libraries.
U1: Shutterstock/oneinchpunch; **U3**: Shutterstock/Alex Staroseltsev; **U4**: Shutterstock/Pavel L Photo and Video; Shutterstock/Anton Kudelin; Shutterstock/Maglara; **U5**: Shutterstock/Matt Gibson; Shutterstock/LoloStock; Shutterstock/LauraDyer; Shutterstock/Panu Ruangjan; Shutterstock/italay; Shutterstock/Roman Malanchuk; Shutterstock/wandee007; Shutterstock/Alek Stemmer; Shutterstock/Tiago M Nunes; **U6**: Shutterstock/Yellowj; Shutterstock/Viacheslav Lopatin; **U7**: Shutterstock/Darren Brode; **U8**: Shuttertsock/wellphoto; U9: Shutterstock/gualtiero boffi; **U10**: Shutterstock/MIMOHE; Shutterstock/marchello74.

Illustrations
Ben Swift; Vicky Woodgate.

Typeset by QBS Learning.

Audio Production by John Marshall Media.

Corpus
Development of this publication has made use of the Cambridge English Corpus (CEC). The CEC is a computer database of contemporary spoken and written English, which currently stands at over one billion words. It includes British English, American English, and other varieties of English. It also includes the Cambridge Learner Corpus, developed in collaboration with the University of Cambridge ESOL Examinations. Cambridge University Press has built up the CEC to provide evidence about language use that helps us to produce better language teaching materials.

English Profile
This product is informed by English Vocabulary Profile, built as part of English Profile, a collaborative program designed to enhance the learning, teaching, and assessment of English worldwide. Its main funding partners are Cambridge University Press and Cambridge Assessment English and its aim is to create a "profile" for English, linked to the Common European Framework of Reference for Languages (CEFR). English Profile outcomes, such as the English Vocabulary Profile, will provide detailed information about the language that learners can be expected to demonstrate at each CEFR level, offering a clear benchmark for learners' proficiency. For more information, please visit www.englishprofile.org.

CALD
The Cambridge Advanced Learner's Dictionary is the world's most widely used dictionary for learners of English. Including all the words and phrases that learners are likely to come across, it also has easy-to-understand definitions and example sentences to show how the word is used in context. The Cambridge Advanced Learner's Dictionary is available online at dictionary.cambridge.org.

CAMBRIDGE
UNIVERSITY PRESS

University Printing House, Cambridge CB2 8BS, United Kingdom

One Liberty Plaza, 20th Floor, New York, NY 10006, USA

477 Williamstown Road, Port Melbourne, VIC 3207, Australia

314–321, 3rd Floor, Plot 3, Splendor Forum, Jasola District Centre, New Delhi – 110025, India

103 Penang Road, #05-06/07, Visioncrest Commercial, Singapore 238467

Cambridge University Press is part of the University of Cambridge.

It furthers the University's mission by disseminating knowledge in the pursuit of education, learning and research at the highest international levels of excellence.

www.cambridge.org
Information on this title: www.cambridge.org/9781108798129

First published 2022
20 19 18 17 16 15 14 13 12 11 10 9 8 7 6 5 4 3 2 1

Printed in Poland by Opolgraf

A catalogue record for this publication is available from the British Library

ISBN 978-1-108-79807-5 Intermediate Student's Book with eBook
ISBN 978-1-108-79679-8 Intermediate Student's Book A with eBook
ISBN 978-1-108-79821-1 Intermediate Student's Book B with eBook
ISBN 978-1-108-86152-6 Intermediate Student's Book with Digital Pack
ISBN 978-1-108-86154-0 Intermediate Student's Book A with Digital Pack
ISBN 978-1-108-86157-1 Intermediate Student's Book B with Digital Pack
ISBN 978-1-108-79812-9 Intermediate Workbook with Answers
ISBN 978-1-108-79813-6 Intermediate Workbook A with Answers
ISBN 978-1-108-79814-3 Intermediate Workbook B with Answers
ISBN 978-1-108-79815-0 Intermediate Workbook without Answers
ISBN 978-1-108-79816-7 Intermediate Workbook A without Answers
ISBN 978-1-108-79817-4 Intermediate Workbook B without Answers
ISBN 978-1-108-79818-1 Intermediate Full Contact with eBook
ISBN 978-1-108-79819-8 Intermediate Full Contact A with eBook
ISBN 978-1-108-79820-4 Intermediate Full Contact B with eBook
ISBN 978-1-108-85951-6 Intermediate Full Contact with Digital Pack
ISBN 978-1-108-85952-3 Intermediate Full Contact A with Digital Pack
ISBN 978-1-108-86153-3 Intermediate Full Contact B with Digital Pack
ISBN 978-1-108-79823-5 Intermediate Teacher's Book with Digital Pack
ISBN 978-1-108-81765-3 Intermediate Presentation Plus

Additional resources for this publication at www.cambridge.org/americanempower